love

how   you

live

ADVENTURES IN INTERIOR DESIGN

love

how   you

live

RODMAN PRIMACK with RUDY WEISSENBERG

HOMES FOR OTHERS

HOMES FOR OURSELVES

Foreword

"You know, I never made this connection," Rudy Weissenberg said to Rodman Primack, his partner of more than two decades, "we both spent a lot of time in those houses, and they were like safe havens." Primack didn't skip a beat. "Oh, I think about it all the time," he said.

Sitting around a sleek glass table inside AGO Projects, the pair's Mexico City–based design practice and gallery, we were talking about their grandmothers—about the homes they put together, or, more precisely, about the easy pleasure with which their lives unfurled within them. In Guatemala City and California, respectively, Weissenberg and Primack found more than refuge inside those domestic settings that mirrored the vivid personalities of their grandmothers. Different aesthetically but both replete with objects collected and cherished for their unique material qualities— things beautiful or bizarre, handcrafted or industrial, made by renowned and anonymous designers alike—the homes were their earliest indicators of how to love how you live. A vase procured from a trip abroad would be topped with flowers freshly picked from the garden, while sunlight traveled throughout the day across richly textured surfaces. Whether simple or elaborate, meals were prepared and enjoyed without fuss. Books and magazines of all sorts were savored cover to cover, providing an amalgam of references through which to cultivate a truly individual sense of self. (This was the time, after all, before algorithms fed us a homogeneously curated set of aspirations.)

It appears that the formative years that Primack and Weissenberg spent inhabiting these idyllic bubbles imprinted in them the value of approaching life with a voracious curiosity, one driven by a honed instinct for finding beauty in the unexpected. Their careers have always been oriented toward design and culture; before they cofounded AGO Projects, Primack was the executive director of Design Miami and of his own design firm and textile house, RP Miller, while Weissenberg was a television producer and exhibition curator. It's unsurprising that the pair are now avid collectors. The six homes that they've designed for themselves over time to fit their nomadic lifestyles each display a unique character, but all reflect an intense fondness for objects, with every room densely populated by art, furniture, textiles, ceramics, glassware, patterned wallpaper, variegated tiles, and countless curios coexisting in eclectic juxtaposition. And while most of those things are possessed of a craftsmanship so exquisite as to make their worth self-evident, others occupy different categories of value, like, say, a charmingly uncanny appearance, an element of whimsy, or a compelling origin story. The latter—the ones that stand as the result and evidence of a maker's extensive experimentation—are perhaps the objects that best reflect the ethos that compels Primack and Weissenberg to accumulate them.

People who inhabit homes so exuberant are often regarded as lively eccentrics, insatiable bon vivants, and there is, of course, a compulsive aspect to collecting. Less explored, however, is the spiritual dimension of it. If collecting is fueled by desire, what fuels the desire itself?

After hours of conversations with Primack and Weissenberg, I began to sense something profound about the way they engage with the world around them. Collecting is not akin to consumerism. In many ways, it is the opposite: an impulse born of deep intention that, for them, doesn't end once they own the things they covet. They want to live with them, touch them, contemplate them, serve food on them, stack them upon each other, sit on them, move them around, watch them age and acquire patina until they become inextricable parts of their lives. Primack has half-joked that this is why they've built so many homes and live in more than one place at once—they're not the type of collectors who would accept stowing their things away in the dark, temperature-controlled rooms of rented storage spaces.

How could they? It would be stunting the energy inherent in the sort of objects they're drawn to, which are imbued with humanity and a spirit of innovation.

Often, the pair don't just purchase these things for themselves. By now, they've deliberately orchestrated professional lives that demand that they take a step further, forming relationships with the artists, designers, and makers, understanding their processes, and supporting their practices. Anyone pushing boundaries or exploring new possibilities in creating represents an opportunity for them to learn, and both Primack and Weissenberg brighten at the mention of this. Championing the work of makers through their platforms, they insist, is far from altruism on their part. In fact, it's such a pleasure that they mostly regard it as self-serving. There's no other way they'd rather spend their days. This is it.

Inevitably, the pair's penchant for storytelling seeps into the homes they design for their clients. There is no tried-and-true formula behind their process, which is why there is also no singular aesthetic binding their work together. Instead, all of their clients' homes stand as tangible assertions of their own personalities, spaces filled with meaningful objects that spin together a narrative of who they are, where they've been, what they're drawn to. If a client is not already enamored with the process of learning about art and design, it's easy to see how they could end up captivated by Primack and Weissenberg's enthusiasm, and their belief that an abode should be an intimate, loving portrait of those who inhabit it. That, ultimately, it should be up to us to decide how we live and what we value.

"I would say that our grandmothers were post-aspirational," Primack told me the day we sat together at their office, overlooking the tops of the jacaranda trees on Reforma Avenue that, just days before, had burst forth in lavender blooms. "Their lives were what they wanted to live and how they wanted to live them." Weissenberg nodded. "And what we learned from them is that they had a very clear vision of who they were," he said. "They had connected to who they were through design."

ANA KARINA ZATARAIN

Love How You Live   Adventures in Interior Design

I have spent most of my life thinking about houses. My sister and I grew up skiing all winter in Sun Valley, Idaho, gratefully returning to Laguna Beach, California, for most of the summer and retreating to the ocean as frequently as possible. As kids of divorce the idea of "home" was not abstract; we actively thought and talked about it. I would design fantasy houses for myself, castles for the characters from *The Wind in the Willows*, and decorate the dream houses of my sister's Barbies—my first-ever commission. The idea of creating a comfortable home meant the world to me.

The houses we actually lived in, my sister and me, were made to measure for our mother and grandmother. They did their own decorating and held wholesale licenses to buy at "trade" prices for themselves and their friends. I grew up thinking it was perfectly normal to source reclaimed wood from a barn and use it as paneling for a ski house (as my mother did), or to use dried wheat stalks to imprint the perfect texture in drying plaster on our walls (as my grandmother did). In California and Idaho alike, we would visit the homes of friends and acquaintances, many of them extraordinary, and I would always go into those experiences with my eyes wide open. Then as now, I loved seeing how other people lived, loved that revealing moment of sudden intimacy, which is itself a kind of knowing. My approach to making and living in homes today distills this whole lifetime's worth of visual, emotional, and sensory experience.

It is, of course, an incredible privilege to grow up this way, and though I vaguely recognized my good luck at points in my childhood, I can't say I fully grasped just how unusual it was to come of age among people who had the time and means to source reclaimed wood from a barn and use it as siding on their ski house, or to hunt down just the right floral chintz for a home in the desert. What I did understand was the singular importance of passion. I grew up around plenty of skiers, sailors, and gardeners but I was always particularly drawn to people who made things, who valued craftsmanship:

cabinetmakers and ceramicists, cooks, bakers, weavers and painters. My understanding of quality and beauty has been shaped by my (possibly outsized) admiration for the handmade, by the respect for material and technique that I learned by imitating and implementing the joyful obsessions modeled by family and friends.

So much of my perspective on design, decorating, and living well is rooted in my past. My love for India's block-printed cottons came from repeated viewings of the BBC miniseries *The Jewel in the Crown* after its 1984 debut. A few years later, at fourteen, I spent a summer in Japan swooning over patterned handmade papers, and Asian-inspired motifs have since appeared time and again in my own textile designs. (I bought so much paper on that trip that I'm still using it to wrap special gifts some thirty years later.) Tile appears in one form or another in almost all our projects; its possibilities have surely stuck with me since the year I spent traveling around Portugal in my teens. I know that I owe at least part of my admiration for contemporary design to the wild, vibrant irreverence of Ettore Sottsass's Esprit stores of the 1980s. My belief in color as a powerful tool for organizing and understanding the world was validated around the same time by a major David Hockney retrospective at LACMA, and my adoration for old wicker, painted floors, mismatched lamps, and threadbare quilts comes from humid lakeside summers in Ontario.

Despite the many joys of these and countless other experiences, I also spent much of my childhood, like so many other gay kids, feeling as though I didn't fit in. Though my sense of isolation was sometimes profound, it could also, at times, be energizing—a generative source that impelled me to escape, travel. When Rudy came into my life over two decades ago, we felt an immediate and profound connection over shared values about the importance of defining home. We kept working to express qualities that made spaces feel rooted, first in our own various homes as we moved from city to city, then

later in the projects we designed together for clients. Our curiosity about other people's lives, about other approaches to living and other ways of being, emerged, in a sense, from shared deep desires to find our own place in the world. And so when we design a home today, it is always with the intention to create a space of safety and joy. Home is where we should be most ourselves.

I'm not relating these experiences here to convince anyone that I can claim any special authority about dictating what's beautiful—quite the opposite. The idea is never to impose a preconceived visual ideal on others, but rather to lead them to their own language for living. It takes time, but it doesn't have to be difficult. Nurture what you love and share that with others. Seek out the beauty in authenticity and minimize your investment in trying to emulate the supposed "good taste" of others. Embrace flexibility and chance, the unresolved and unexpected. These principles work in decorating because they work in life.

RODMAN PRIMACK

thacher

↦ OJAI

My first-ever clients—discounting, of course, my sister's pioneering Barbie dolls—were a couple, Anne and Dudley DeZonia. They had a beautiful neo-Regency house from 1928 maintained, unusually for Southern California, in pristine condition. Though Anne and Dudley and I come from different generations, we all have deep roots in California. Dudley grew up next door to my mother—unbelievably, we found this out only after we'd started to work together—in the Quaker community of Whittier, famous for having given us M.F.K. Fisher and infamous for Nixon. Anne's father, meanwhile, had been the first city judge in Santa Monica, where she grew up. With our shared histories, we were able to take the kind of risks that have since, I think, come to define my practice. We hired David Wiseman, recently out of RISD, to spend nearly a year on a scaffold, installing the first of the plaster-and-porcelain ceilings that have since become his calling card. We shopped at flea markets and auction houses. Anne and Dudley found a bundle of exquisite antique *sudare* in Japan, which I used to make my ideal bathroom shades. And I designed my first textile—a floral pattern based on Iznik tiles—for the curtains of their generous sitting room. That house shaped me; there are few projects I've loved more. And so it's fitting that my most recent project would bring the three of us back together, this time in Ojai, one of the few places left in Southern California that even my grandmother might recognize. ↵ The Ojai basin is a blessed place, a quiet agricultural valley ringed by the Topatopa Mountains about ten miles inland from the Pacific. The whole valley still smells of orange blossoms, and the hills flush pink each evening when the sun sinks below the horizon. So many American vacation towns (I won't name them, but you can guess which) have fallen into a careless kind of placelessness, shaped as they are by extravagant wealth unconstrained by a rooted community. Ojai is not that kind of place. ↵ Here, in the heart of this old California, the DeZonias found a clapboard farmhouse from 1890 surrounded by twenty acres of citrus, avocado, and oak. Now formally protected as a historic landmark, the house had undergone some unfortunate renovations in the early 1980s—unnecessary room divisions, an unthinkable wall-to-wall white shag carpet—that we needed to erase. To make those changes, we brought on the architect Odom Stamps, a New Orleans native who brings that city's inherent instinct for the good life to everything he does. And though Anne and Dudley were, of course, committed to restoring the house to its original state, none us wanted a stuffy period-perfect interior. This was California, after all, which means so many things to so many people, but for us fundamentally suggests a place where beauty is easy and "nice" things—surely a concept imported from the fusty East Coast—could sit coolly alongside a pair of dirty shoes, muddy from an afternoon spent picking figs. It meant nostalgia, yes, but nostalgia for a place that has always stubbornly (and perhaps naively) turned its face toward the future, squinting blindly into the boundless sun. ↵ At its heart and at its best, California is all about the generative spirit of cultures and traditions that clash and blend with gleeful abandon. The Los Angeles of my childhood was a city of pastiche, a place where mock Tudors, Cape Cods, craftsman bungalows, and Monterrey Mission–style mansions sat unselfconsciously on the same aspirational block and where big neon signs advertised "Lox and Chow Mein" in the San Gabriel Valley. California is a place where subcultures—surfers, hippies, Hollywood types, tech types—evolve, for better and sometimes for worse, into entire ways of being. The Ojai house would encapsulate *those* Californias as well as our many shared passions: for entertaining, for art, for objects; for travel and clothes and food and gardens. I would gladly live in this house myself. The view from the front porch, looking out over miles of orange groves to the distant Sierra Madre, is what comes reflexively to mind whenever I miss California, which is often. Designing this house has been an almost Proustian exercise, full of McGuire bamboo furniture—de rigueur for any house that my grandmother and her friends would have deemed "pretty" (high praise)—and original pool chaises from the Beverly Hills Hotel. ↵ There's a touch of sentimentality to it all, but it's not only that. The contemporary artist Francesca DiMattio made a neo-baroque porcelain chandelier for the dining room, along with an extraordinary fireplace mantle and sconces. David Wiseman is currently working on an immersive installation for the powder room, the young Mexican design office Paraphernalia made us a suite of outdoor furniture to place under the pergola. Anne's dear friend in Paris, Marie Christophe, made an extraordinary beaded pagoda lantern for the garden cabana. There are antique Delft tiles in the kitchen and a hooked Portuguese rug for the master bedroom and yards of vintage Le Manach printed cottons for the guest room. A bronze nymph by the artist Claude Lalanne, which we acquired together all those years ago for the first house in Hancock Park, has traveled the long distance to Ojai to look over the patio, a guardian from our shared past. The whole thing is warm and gentle and inclusive, worldly but modest—a place of abundance for these lifelong Californians who love nothing more than to feel the fertile earth firmly below their feet.

An Ed Ruscha watercolor and Hugo the puppy welcome visitors. A large terracotta MyungJin Kim vessel rests atop an antique
English Arts and Crafts table from the collection of François Catroux.

A rare vintage tramp art cabinet, contemporary Venetian glass table designed by Marie-Rose Kahane, and pair of vintage T.H. Robsjohn-Gibbings sofas placed back-to-back in the sitting room offer plenty of texture.

A group of herbarium specimens from the famed collection of Bernard Bertrand was the starting point for the dining room. New York–based Francesca DiMattio was commissioned to make the ceramic chandelier.

Francesca DiMattio was also tasked with making the exuberant ceramic mantel and sconces in the principal bedroom.

The owners collect art from both Africa and Oceania, including this beaded chair,
which rests below an embroidered piece by Sophia Narrett.

19   Almost unintentionally, vintage pieces by T.H. Robsjohn-Gibbings found their way to the
sitting room, including a pair of sofas, coffee table, and armchair.

An existing collection of vintage Italian trompe l'oeil plates was expanded to fill the breakfast room wall.

Antique Delft tiles sourced at auction and from dealers create a stove surround.

Vibrant vintage chintz discovered at friend Peter Dunham's warehouse was one of the first textiles purchased for the project. The op art rug was made in Mexico by Pedro y Juana.

An office tucked into an upstairs dormer features a cheerful Lake August nasturtium-print linen on the walls and Roman shade.

Local ceramacist Rebekah Miles designed guest bathroom tiles to include the flora and fauna of Ojai.   thacher ↦ OJAI

Great things found by the owners were waiting for us at the start of the project, like a box of antique cream and green Minton tiles.

An RP Miller blanket woven in Guatemala hangs over the foot of the vintage bamboo four-poster bed.

An antique Anglo-Indian ebony chair with bone inlay made its way from Hancock Park to live below antique Indian bird paintings.

thacher ↦ OJAI

Leah O'Connell's Grace print is edged in a rickrack trim for the bunk room.
Custom sheets featured throughout the house were embroidered in Portugal based on Rodman's designs.

31

A Napoleone Martinuzzi cast-glass sconce in the butler's pantry gives another pair in the sitting room a little vintage company.

The bronze fountain Olympe by Claude Lalanne watched over the first house we did with these clients twenty years ago; she seems even happier now in Ojai.

thacher ↦ OJAI

The young Mexico-based design studio Parafernalia designed the outdoor tables and chairs.

Local artist Ian Collings made the carved red stone piece for the space above the mantel.   thacher ↦ OJAI

The deep, inviting front porch is watched over by a bronze bust of Anne made by a good friend, the author and illustrator Ian Falconer.

thacher ↦ OJAI

Everything that the New York–based contemporary American artist Francesca DiMattio produces makes us question what we think we knew about supposedly well-defined forms of art. From her large-scale paintings to ambitious ceramic assemblages that seem to meld ready-made discarded antique China sets, extruded clay hair, Sicilian *putti*, and ancient sculptures, she twists recognizable media into visual tropes full of unexpected layers and crashing patterns. It's a challenge to established ideas about beauty and aesthetics in general. This makes her work beautiful, but in no traditional sense of the word. We were introduced to Francesca through our good friend and frequent collaborator Jeanne Greenberg Rohatyn many years ago; now she works with another great gallerist friend, Nina Johnson. We were immediately smitten by these huge, precarious-seeming pieces, which often look as though they might topple at any moment but are actually muscular and dainty simultaneously. The work focuses on contrasts, pushing the boundaries of what *can* be combined into a composition, however abstract, and ultimately finding balance—but without any reliance on symmetry. ↩ Francesca grew up with an artist mother who was likewise dedicated to ceramics, then went on to receive an MFA from Columbia University in 2005. Though so much of her work is in clay, Francesca would not consider herself a ceramicist; she inhabits an artistic space originally carved out by fellow artist Betty Woodman, who determined that her ceramics were not vessels, they were artworks that *could* serve as vessels, but function came secondary to artistic intent. So much about contemporary art is context, or how the artist positions the work they are creating. Often the medium is simply a way to explore an idea, but the medium is usually not the defining feature of the work itself. Recent collaborations with Francesca, from an entire ceramic mantelpiece to wall sconces and a chandelier for our citrus farm project in Ojai, California, feel like they're upending eighteenth-century trompe l'œil— where she is tricking the eye into believing that her pieces have been assembled from broken pieces of ceramics from different periods and locations. Some of the patterns are lyrical variations of classic Sèvres, Nymphenburg, Imari, Delft, and Wedgwood motifs; some are common thrift-store patterns. What appears to be random mixing, you realize upon gazing at her work, is actually the result of a studied and cautious specificity. ↩ Ornament has proven essential to the human expression of culture for centuries. Ideas about how much ornament constitutes "good taste" and what types of ornament are either high design or primitive have shifted through time and region, have been adopted, adapted, or eventually discarded. Francesca's work explores the contradictions in how ornament can both conceal or enhance. Delicate, detailed ceramic flowers act structurally on one piece while rougher, abstracted blooms might serve as purely surface decoration. It's this play of contradictions, this refutation of the current fascination with minimalism, the complete disregard for the typical "good taste" of today that makes her work so attractive and compelling and Francesca such an exciting artist.

REBEKAH MILES ↦ OJAI

So often we find that objects we love, objects that elicit an emotional response, have been made by people who likewise elicit emotions in us as well. The most special things, in short, are made by special people. There is something so wonderful in recognizing that emotion can be captured in an object of art, and that we can then import that emotion directly into our life or home. ↵ Rebekah Miles is a ceramicist working from her home studio nestled in a bucolic wooded canyon midway between Ojai and Carpinteria, just inland from the Pacific Ocean. She grew up on this piece of land among the native oak, sycamore, madrone, and manzanita trees that form the quintessential landscapes of this part of California, and of course there are cultivated groves of citrus and avocado just steps away. There are also beds of nasturtiums and geraniums sheltering baby bunnies and squirrels. This is pastoral living at its zenith, and it is captured lyrically in Rebekah's charming work. Although she doesn't set out to memorialize or glorify California, the fact that she grew up and works on a ranch that has been in her extended family for seven generations clearly plays a role in explaining why her pieces feel so effortless and right—she is so imbued with place that she transcribes it naturally. Each piece speaks of her own history and connection to the nature that surrounds her. In Rebekah's hands, plates, jugs, and candlesticks take on an elusive, timeless quality; some feel like they could have been forgotten on a bar shelf at a 1940s pier restaurant, others could have been displayed prominently in a great-grandmother's curio cabinet, while still others feel right at home in a downtown loft. There is something direct and inviting about her hand-painted wares. The pieces are delicate and unfussy, beautiful, whimsical, and earthy. All these seemingly contradictory elements add up to perfection. ↵ Rebekah started painting regularly in the late 1990s while studying at Scripps College, the esteemed women's school not far from Los Angeles. She continued her art studies in the MFA program at Portland State University in Oregon. Later, in 2008, she started teaching herself ceramics and returned to the ranch in 2016 with her young daughter, Inez, in tow. Her small, shaded studio is a few steps from her simple home, parts of which were built in the 1800s. Her process is slow and laborious. Each piece takes time to fashion from large clay slabs. First come molds, then drying, bisque firing, painting, glazing, and firing again. The time commitment is significant and is why she calls her pieces "contemporary heirlooms." Despite this moniker, most of Rebekah's pieces are meant to be used in a quotidian fashion, and she hopes that although collectors consider them special, they won't lock them up behind glass or in a cupboard. They are invitations to bring a little graciousness to each day. Of course, cereal and berries taste infinitely better eaten out of one of her bowls.

las tortugas

↪ HAWAII

As a little kid I told anyone who would listen that, when I grew up, I was going to be an architect—a profession that, to my fantastical imagination, implied a hefty dose of interior design as well as botany and some kind of art practice on the side. I often spent hours toiling happily over imagined floor plans and elevations, laying out complex gardens that radiated outward from elaborate fountains and dreaming up fanciful bathrooms and ballrooms on spaceships—only the essentials, of course, in my whimsical vision of the future. ↩ At a certain point in my teens, I got spooked by the "math" involved and all the fastidious work at the computer. It has instead been one of the great pleasures of my adult life to work closely with artist-technicians who make my abandoned dreams their own professional reality. I am endlessly delighted by the way that architects organize information, ideas, and what they call "program," or the nuts and bolts of how spaces work and how they come together to make a building. Hiring an architect and interior designer together—when the two are compatible, of course—and giving them equal respect and weight, opens enviable opportunities to create rooms and truly memorable properties that are unified by a clearly defined set of values, a coherent sensibility. A well-executed shared vision is something you can feel from the moment you walk into a space. ↩ Among the most fruitful relationships of my professional life has been the one I've fostered with the Seattle-based architect Tom Kundig, which began in 2007 during our collaboration on this marvelous beach house on the Kona Coast of Hawaii's Big Island. Beyond the sheer quality of the architectural design—sensitivity to landscape, precision craftsmanship,

formal sincerity combined with technical sophistication—I'm consistently amazed by the warmth and openness that Tom and his team bring to every interaction. He's told me more than once that I push him out of his comfort zone; for me, his clarity of purpose is a constant reminder that the simplest solution is almost invariably the best one. Here in Hawaii, that philosophy manifests in hinged shutters that open up, rather than out, over the garden cabana and the wooden walkways that traverse the property, not in contrived meanders conceived for the sake of theatrics, but direct lines from point A to point B. There's a humble question that Tom repeats often and that I should really embroider on a throw pillow as a reminder that it should be my personal axiom: What would a farmer do? It's the only interrogatory you need in the face of nearly any design conundrum. Efficiency, elegance, economy—these are the hallmarks not only of Tom's work but of utilitarian, vernacular architecture and design everywhere. ↩ Our deep consensus would have been meaningless, of course, without the enthusiasm and trust of our clients. Family-oriented people with a profound love for entertaining—hence the scale of this project, set as a sequence of four wooden pavilions arranged among gardens—these clients are also attentive, decisive, and communicative. They offered encouragement whenever they could, exhibited constant respect and admiration for the entire team, and, on the occasions when they were disappointed by a decision or outcome, knew how to express it without drama or recrimination. Collaboration goes beyond the so-called "creatives" behind a project's design. Successful projects include everyone. We all knew this project represented a special opportunity—it's not every day that an architect and designer get to design every last element down to dishes and glassware—and we treated one another with proportionate respect. Farmers cultivate. That process requires patience, know-how, and, every once in a while, a bit of ruthlessness. It also requires love.

An exceptional David Wiseman branch chandelier joins a rare vintage Wendell Castle chair, Jean Royère standing lamp/table
and Rick Owens daybed.

A photograph by Lola Schnabel dominates the guesthouse sitting room.
The heavy indigo linen fabric on the daybed was quilted to mimic moving blankets.

Contemporary art, vintage collectible furniture, and widely sourced textiles ground each bedroom.
A tapestry by Fernanda Brunet, left, and a unique photograph by Tierney Gearon, right, add to the mix.

las tortugas ⊦ HAWAII

A circa 1956 freestanding closet/room divider by Le Corbusier and Charlotte Perriand
defines the principal dressing room.

Brazilian sculptor/designer Hugo França searched for a year for the perfect tree
to make the pool bridge.   las tortugas ↦ HAWAII

A "napping" hut by Atelier Van Lieshout and a pair of vintage Stefan Zwicky concrete LC2 chairs offer accommodation on the lawn.

las tortugas ↦ HAWAII

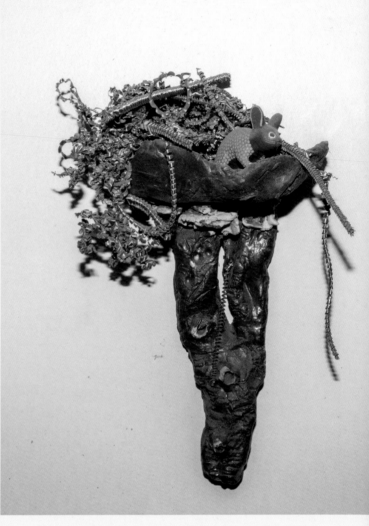

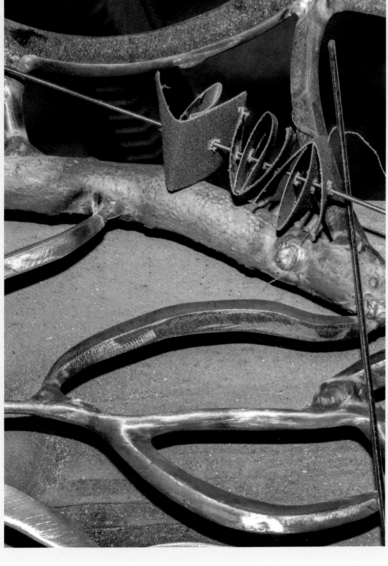

Our relationship with David has been one of the most fruitful in our history, both in terms of project collaborations and personal friendships. We met him in his Brooklyn studio thanks to an introduction by his brother Ari shortly after he graduated from the Rhode Island School of Design in the early aughts. It wasn't long after the meeting that David accepted a commission for a plaster-and-porcelain cherry blossom ceiling for Anne Crawford and Dudley DeZonia's 1928 Hancock Park home by Roland E. Coate. It would result in a year's work—much of it recumbent on scaffolding—but it also returned him home permanently to his native Los Angeles. The piece was an immediate sensation that led to many more collaborations together and, most significantly, the establishment of David's much-lauded and prolific practice designing lighting, furniture, sculpture, and decorative objects. ↩ Today, David has an impressive studio complex (and is business partners with Ari) in Frogtown, a neighborhood full of artists just northwest of downtown L.A., along the banks of the recently restored Los Angeles River. There, he creates everything from major site-specific room environments in bronze, porcelain, glass, enamel, precious stones, terrazzo, and countless other innovative and traditional materials to intimately scaled candlesticks or pill boxes. David's love of nature influences almost every piece; he has created his own clear visual language that combines elements of the natural world around him to generate assemblages that project familiar elements of plants we recognize without being strict imitations of natural forms—for example, in a recent commission, porcelain-and-bronze wisteria blossoms cascade from a ceiling, but at a scale that is much larger than life. This playfulness, this ability to skew reality, is partly what gives his work such energy and depth—things are at once recognizable yet clearly artistic interpretations. David cites inspiration from great masters of the Wiener Werkstätte, such as Josef Hoffmann and Dagobert Peche, as well as a fascination with patternmaking across cultures. He mixes forms, textures, and materials with riotous abandon. His goal is to make something beautiful, fanciful, beguiling, and engaging, not necessarily "true".
↩ Collectors are drawn to the work of David Wiseman because of the fundamental beauty in each piece and the clear marks of the skillful handling of material. The studio even feels like a contemporary version of renowned ateliers of the past, like Louis Comfort Tiffany's revived. This is not to mean that the work is historicist or revivalist, too influenced by the past; on the contrary, it is actually comes from a place of great confidence and intuitive understanding about contemporary life and our need to be stimulated by beauty and to feel the joy of wonder in the twenty-first century. Pleasure and tactility are more necessary than ever in our everyday existence.

DAVID WISEMAN ⇥ PASADENA

When lit, a Studio Wieki Somers standing lamp casts beautiful shadows in a corner of the sitting room.

greenwich village

↦ N Y C

I am comfortable in New York City, but I'm a Californian at heart. I would say I'm always happy to pass time on the East Coast, while Rudy falls easily into being a New Yorker and is genuinely most himself in this dense, tightly wound city. This apartment marked a return for us; the previous time we'd lived in New York together, our home had become a kind of homage to the life we'd actually shared in London—we had imported an inward-looking atmosphere, cozy from drizzle and gray. By the time we found this place on 10th Street, in 2014, though, I felt very ready to tackle New York again, both physically and emotionally. It's true that, between us, this time, we had a goal of creating a home that would speak in the language of the city it was in: frenetic and confident and brash. ↵ The apartment had its structural quirks. It was long and narrow, but also had exceptionally high ceilings and big, south-facing windows (partially blocked by air-conditioning units). But we sensed immediately how to make it work and had the design for the remodel ready within days. I'd just been in Milan for the Salone del Mobile, too, where I saw a presentation of a new terrazzo-like engineered material called Marmoreal created by the English designer Max Lamb for my former colleague Brent Dzorckius's company, Dzek. By the time we closed on the apartment just a few weeks later, we were already ordering slabs of this new nougat full of bright chips of colored marble to tile our new bathrooms. The process was fluid and easy—a clear sign that we were both ready for this change. ↵ We'd already identified several artworks that we knew we wanted to live with, so we designed the project to maximize display space even in unconventional places, like the kitchen. We also chose to sacrifice a wall that seemed like an intuitive place for a gallery display and converted it to shelving. We (or, rather I—Rudy would say I have a problem in this particular arena) tend to accumulate books with greedy zeal. We commissioned our friend and frequent collaborator, the gifted Brooklyn-based metal whisperer Gabrielle Shelton, to build the most incredible set of steel bookshelves. They seem to float over the wall without any visible support, though Gab has told me there's enough structural steel embedded in the wall that I could climb the shelves like a ladder. ↵ Rudy and I are always trying to remove the hierarchies we see regularly imposed on objects. That means humble burlap cloth is promoted to a wall covering and a fitting backdrop for artworks by John Armleder and Wolfgang Tillmans. It means ceramics picked up at flea markets are placed next to bronze bowls by Alma Allen on an experimental carbon fiber coffee table by Jonathan Muecke. Beautiful things are deemed beautiful when we decide they are, not when a brand manager or trend predictor makes a pronouncement. We always want people to feel a real connection to the objects that surround them, to their intrinsic qualities and history. We want them to feel that those objects are extensions of themselves. ↵ Placing our books as a focal point of our home—these volumes that both truly contain and symbolically represent so much of our accumulated experience and knowledge—was a way for us to highlight what matters most to us. I love that this prominent feature of our home, which also provides its central structure, is, ultimately, a tool to help us organize and access our library. It delights me to my core when something so utilitarian can also be so gorgeous, can embody so perfectly that auspicious dialogue between function and pleasure. It's about as fine a goal as I can imagine for any home.

Jim Lambie's portrait of David Bowie watches over a Milena Muzquiz ceramic sculpture.

A custom Fedora Design hand-creweled wool rug was a wedding gift from the designer Federica Tondato.

Walls for art by Tom Burr, Wolfgang Tillmans, and Jack Early, from left to right.

The room's unique vessels include Alma Allen's bronze bowls and Floris Wubben's ceramic pots.

Rodman's grandmother's Noni's vintage cloisonné boxes atop
a Roger Capron ceramic table.

RP Miller textile Perry's Arrows envelops the principal bedroom.   greenwich village ↦ NYC

Max Lamb's Marmoreal, a terrazzo-like stone, clads every surface of the bath.

A big pinch of art spices up the kitchen, including pieces by Kendell Geers,
Konstantin Kakanias, and Assume Vivid Astro Focus, from left to right.

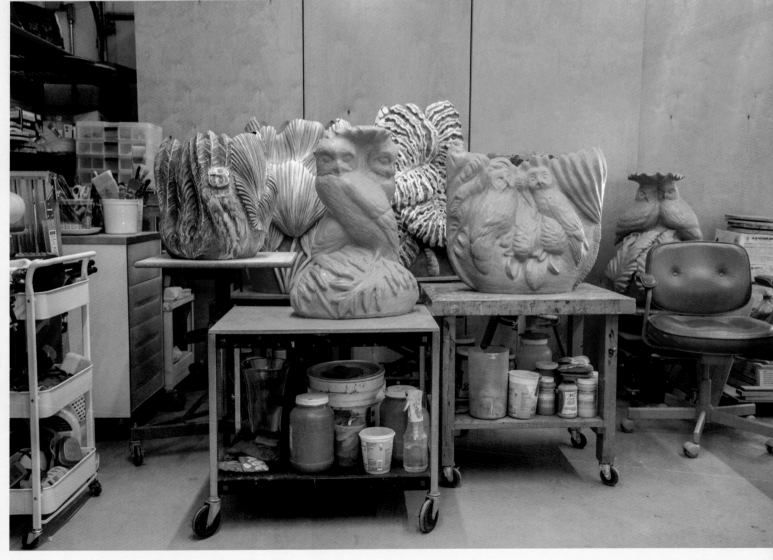

Chance encounters can truly alter a life's course, and meeting MyungJin Kim felt like one of those moments for us. She visited Mexico City with her partner, the renowned artist and ceramist Tony Marsh, alongside the founders of Nonaka-Hill Gallery, Taka and Rodney. Their visit coincided with art week in Mexico, and as is customary, we began following each other on social media, establishing a rapport centered around art and design. ↵ A couple of months later, MJ started posting work that simply mesmerized us. She explained that the trip to Mexico had inspired her to use terra cotta, creating vessels that were slightly rough, graphic. Her work showcased recurring themes of owls and prehistoric plants, drawing inspiration from the garden she and Tony had cultivated at home—a garden adorned with specimens he had collected over decades. This shift in her work also marked a personal pivot; MJ was embarking on a new life in Southern California with Tony after spending two years at the renowned Archie Bray Foundation in Montana, honing her skills and developing her craft. The change in her personal life translated into a burst of new artistic energy. ↵ Her previous work had been characterized by precision and intricacy, and pieces were often in smaller-scale white porcelain, featuring themes such as caged birds. It felt a bit traditional, influenced by export porcelain from Asia that was highly collected and appreciated in Europe in the eighteenth century. While technically impressive, the new work also symbolized a release—both from an unhealthy prior relationship and from the constraints of small porcelain vessels. MJ was now hand-building large and technically complicated terra cotta vessels that conveyed newfound freedom for her ideas and, evidently, for herself. ↵ These towering vessels, sometimes taller than MJ herself, begin as low-relief sculptures with white slip-painted details. They transform into three-dimensional sculptures, painted and polished with terra sigillata. MJ works with an intensity that borders on compulsion, laboring until her hands ache, demonstrating a focus and a clear vision for each piece from its inception—no small feat when considering their weight, scale, and need to balance. ↵ Together, we have presented her work in more than half a dozen exhibitions across the U.S. and Europe and have embarked on commissions for interior projects. One collaboration resulted in the creation of wall tapestries with the same subject matter as the vessels, another two super-scaled sculptures for our recent Hacienda Los Milagros project, with the pieces displayed in nine-foot niches. The evolution of MJ's work continues to captivate and inspire us. ↵ Visiting MJ and Tony's house in California is an enormous treat. She is also great in the kitchen (creatives tend to be multitalented) and usually makes a Korean meal with a perfectly calibrated strong coffee. Sitting on the back porch, in the garden that connects the house to their home studio, is an enjoyable and meaningful experience where we discuss, among many things, avenues to unleash her creativity. It is sitting on that porch when we have come up with ideas for exhibitions, projects, and new pieces.

Mono Rojo began as a didactic experiment—a ceramic studio with a focus on crafting utilitarian objects for Japanese restaurants in and around Mexico City. Founded by two friends, Mexican artist Olmo Uribe and Japanese potter Hiroshi Okuno, the studio set up a kiln in a townhouse in the storied Santa Maria la Ribera area. They started producing delicate pieces that quickly gained a devoted following. They swiftly established its signature style—a proprietary blend of clays that are rich, tactile, and adorned with idiosyncratic hand paintings and clear glazes. Today, the studio stands as one of the most prolific ceramic companies in the city, and has evolved into a rich collective of artists all working under the name Mono Rojo. Theirs is a creative collaboration that values the process as much as the end result. No individual artist claims credit for a specific piece, and often multiple artists contribute to a single creation. ↩ Ceramics demand creativity, technique, patience, and a bit of luck. Many ceramists incorporate a good luck charm in each firing, adding a touch of superstition to the mix of experience. At Mono Rojo, the loading and opening of the kiln become moments of joy and anticipation—a ritual in itself. The unpredictable reactions of the fire gods to the clay offerings make the kiln-opening experience both joyous and occasionally disappointing. The pieces crafted by Mono Rojo project a sense of seeming improvisation, but the creation process is anything but random. Tasks are democratically divided among the group; some artists prefer wheel throwing, while others enjoy hand building and painting. Multiple pieces are typically in various stages of creation, and the drying racks provide a tantalizing preview of their newest directions. ↩ We frequently visit the studio to immerse ourselves in inspiration and witness the diverse shapes and ideas emerging from the artists. While we love to engage in discussions about possible creative directions and general ideas, we respect the artists' autonomy. For our collaborative projects, we've encouraged the studio to explore larger scales and venture into decorative objects such as lamps, tables, even drums that double as stools. We bring references and inspirations—often vintage images—and delight in the joyous and fresh perspective the studio infuses into each piece. Their creations can effortlessly add a touch of joy to any room—the real goal of Mono Rojo.

Panamanian architect Johann Wolfschoon designed this elongated sofa.
A large piece by Dario Escobar hangs above.

montebello

Rudy and I moved to Guatemala City, his hometown, in 2014 so that he could help with the family business. When we first arrived, we settled into his old room at his mother, Annelie's, sprawling, U-shaped home. Much to my mother-in-law's delight, we stayed. Guatemala City sits about 5,000 feet above sea level, in a valley surrounded by mountains and volcanoes. Annelie's house overlooks the city from the edge of the basin, and the first time I visited, twenty-five years ago, two volcanoes erupted simultaneously in the middle of the night, clearly visible through the large window in my room. It was primordial and intoxicating—I half expected dinosaurs to storm through the garden. The earth here reminds us that it's fully alive. It shakes and trembles and several times a year is covered in a blanket of ash. Spit a watermelon seed into the dirt and you'll see sprouts in a matter of days.   ↩   It's all too common, sadly, for places still rich with traditional local know-how to value what comes from abroad over what's made at home. It was important to us to break with that attitude—and easy, too, surrounded as we are here by so many beautiful handmade things. We patched together a carpet from wool textiles woven on waist looms in the Mayan highlands and used wood that had been curing at the family sawmill for over three decades. A brilliant local metalsmith spent the better part of a year making us window casings and doors, shelving, benches, and side tables. We made a point of seeking out a workshop that still produced the handmade ceramic and cement tiles that were once common here but fell out of fashion ages ago, then commissioned Dario Escobar, a contemporary artist and architect from the city, to design tiles that we used on floors and walls throughout the house.   ↩   We avoided importing wherever possible. Much of our furniture and kitchenware is inherited from Rudy's grandmother, who left stacks of Finnish dinnerware and enameled Dansk bowls and amazing Vera Neumann linens. A committed modernist, she'd filled her house with leather Soriana sofas designed in the 1970s by Afra and Tobia Scarpa and lighting by Achille Castiglioni. Combining these twentieth-century pieces with Guatemalan crafts gave them new life and new context. Rather than overwhelming the space with too many colors and materials, we settled on a few that we loved and allowed the house itself to transform them depending on where they were placed, how the light hit them, and the atmosphere of each different room. If we wanted something and couldn't find it, we had it made—one of the deepest joys of working in places still populated with skilled artisans. We made lighting and hardware, cabinet pulls and doorstops, often figuring out what we needed only as the renovation evolved. When designing for ourselves, we love nothing more than leaving space for accident and surprise, for spontaneous and often joyful solutions to unexpected problems.   ↩   We don't spend as much time as we might like at this home in Guatemala, though going to bed in our hillside cloud and waking up to clear skies and views across the valley remains one of the greatest joys in our sometimes-chaotic lives. On a recent Christmas holiday, we hunkered down here for ten days. In that time, I left the house all of twice. You can't give a house a bigger compliment: it should offer calm, refuge, a place to be with yourself and the things you love.

A Gabriel Kuri tapestry and a vintage Charlotte Perriand oak-and-rush armchair
accent the home's public spaces.

Red-painted Assume Vivid Astro Focus stools feature seats made of Rio de Janeiro sidewalk pavers.

Cement tiles throughout the house are by Guatemalan artist Darío Escobar.

The bedroom's pair of monoprints are by Guatemalan artist Naufus Ramírez-Figueroa.

An early painting by Roberto Ossay, Rudy's great-uncle.

A vintage chair covered in RP Miller textile Chiyo's Pond.

north fork

↦ LONG ISLAND

Long Island's bucolic North Fork is, geographically speaking, just a short distance away from the mansions and gardens of the Hamptons and Sag Harbor—but spiritually it's another universe. Working farms and fishing villages still thrive here, and windswept dunes roll lazily into the water. This house—a shingled Dutch Colonial Revival with a gambrel roof and tidy procession of dormers—sits on a particularly spectacular lot at the narrowest point on the peninsula. It's a spit of land, an isthmus barely 1,500 feet across, and it separates Long Island Sound from Gardiners Bay. It's an island on an island, isolated and dramatic. ↩ Though this North Fork house had beautiful lines and an incomparable setting, its interior was fractured and disjointed thanks to years of patchwork renovations. And so, working closely with our clients and the architect Tom Kundig—the second time we came together in this particular three-sided configuration—we gutted the building while leaving its timeless exterior intact. (Tom also designed a typically discreet annex to make space for guests and added a six-by-six Jean Prouvé demountable house to be used as an office.) We didn't want to call

attention to our interventions. We also weren't interested in slavish obedience to a particular period or style. ↩ By the time we started this project in 2013, we'd been working with these clients—a warm, generous, gregarious family—for almost a decade, so benefited from a professional relationship built on the many years of friendship that preceded it. We've even vacationed together, allowing Rudy and me to experience firsthand the way they live in and use their spaces, both their Tribeca apartment and the Hawaii compound. We'd spent years collecting together, too, assembling masterworks by luminaries of twentieth-century design such as Joaquim Tenreiro and José Zanine Caldas. They've been interested in Brazil's midcentury efflorescence from the beginning—and later Finn Juhl and Edward Wormley, Jean Prouvé and Mathieu Matégot, sometimes accumulating pieces early enough in the project that they would go on to inform the architecture itself. ↩ Working with clients over the course of many years opens endless possibilities to identify what they need and want and to begin collecting objects and ideas long before a new project begins. ↩ Thanks to our long history together, we had time, for instance, to find the perfect dining table—in this case a long, graceful piece designed in the 1950s by the great Charlotte Perriand, one of tragically few female voices admitted into the canon of twentieth-century designers. Here, too, there are multiple important works by Jean Royère, including a pair of canopied lounge chairs, and very rare Joseph-André Motte chairs with patchwork "harlequin" leather seats. David Wiseman designed incredible bronze screens and fireplace tools for the soaring concrete hearths at either end of the two-story great room. There really isn't a corner or moment in this house that isn't imbued with provenance and intention. They are also all thoroughly used—vitally and vividly lived in. Finding the right client, or, maybe more accurately, being found by them, is nothing short of alchemy.

Haas Brothers ceramics sit atop a sideboard by South African designers Dokter and Misses, and below a drawing by Thomas Houseago.

Vintage Edward Wormley sofas were reupholstered in RP Miller textiles embroidered by Irma Baján.

A Mitchell Denburg for RP Miller rug rests below a special Jean Royère canopied chair and a custom fire screen and set of fireplace tools by David Wiseman.

Rodman designed the RP Miller Nezu textile for this room, and used it on both the daybed and shades.

A large Takuro Kuwata ceramic piece in the window echoes the colors on the vintage faux ikat fabric that covers a pair of armchairs.

A quilted nook provides an extra sleeping and reading spot in the guest house.

A group of vintage paper Akari lanterns by Isamu Noguchi, originally sold
by Steph Simon, become functional sculpture in the media room.

north fork ↦ LONG ISLAND

A circa 1969 Wendell Castle fiberglass Cloud shelf provides space for a display of whimsical objects above this seating area.

107 This bedroom is endowed with Marthe Armitage's Hop Garden hand-blocked wallpaper
and an Elizabeth Peyton aquatint portrait of Georgia O'Keeffe.

A rare vintage Wendell Castle plinth/room divider and Haas Brothers "beasts" bring sculpture and texture to this bedroom.

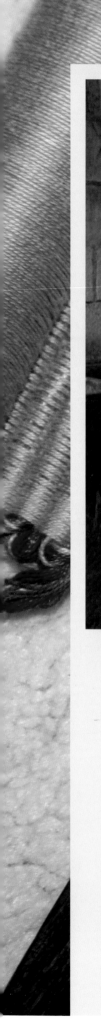

We began our collaboration with Irma Baján and her family over a decade ago, when we were seeking out skilled embroiderers in Guatemala for our fabric projects. Our connection was established through Vey Smithers, the formidable founder of Colibrí, an esteemed textile shop in Antigua, Guatemala, that creates work for almost five hundred female Guatemalan artisans. While hand embroidery has been largely replaced by machines, we believe that the spirit of handmade work brings a unique depth, complexity, and beauty to fabrics that machines cannot replicate. It imparts a sense of individuality that sets handmade pieces apart and carries energy from the maker. ↵ Irma resides in Patzún, a small town in the Guatemalan highlands, about two hours from the capital. In her community, most individuals are either involved in agriculture or dedicate their lives to weaving and embroidery. Having grown up and married there, Irma chose to follow her calling in textiles as well. She has passed on her skills to her daughters and can collaborate with a network of women when the workload is substantial. The economics of the industry pose challenges, requiring Irma and her family to work nearly twelve hours a day to make ends meet. Irma is divorced now, but also cares for her sister's children, making her responsible for providing for a household of six individuals. Their home, a three-story house, serves as the backdrop for their intensive and physically demanding work.

Back-strapped looms are scattered throughout the house, each always in various stages of production, alongside three embroidery stations handling multiple projects simultaneously. ↵ An entrepreneur at heart, Irma has sought innovative avenues for selling her creations; she cultivated enduring relationships with the textile museum in Guatemala City and Colibrí in Antigua. She develops unique pieces for both establishments and is constantly coming up with new ideas. To cope with market demands and the low prices of traditional cloth, Irma has adapted her craft, moving away from the traditional monthlong process of crafting *huipils* (colorful traditional blouses worn by women) to creating towels, napkins, placemats, and tablecloths. Her pieces are vibrant, intricate, and sophisticated. She takes a collaborative approach with clients to develop distinctive patterns and shapes. ↵ We have commissioned Irma and her daughters to embroider on fabrics mostly designed by Rodman. Together, we conceive simple, graphic ideas relevant to a specific project. Extensive effort goes into developing drawings and testing colorways, scale, and patterns. While subtle, the handmade nature of these creations is unmistakable, drawing people to appreciate these unique pieces that carry the touch of skilled craftsmanship, even to the untrained eye.

IRMA BAJAN ↦ GUATEMALA

Mitch Denburg, a spirited adventurer and a devoted textile enthusiast, embarked on a transformative journey that wound up shaping his career in unexpected ways. Hailing from New Jersey, he set out as a budding—albeit financially strapped—photographer in 1977 to explore the Yucatán Peninsula and capture black-and-white images for reproduction and sale in the United States. His vision was to establish his name in portraiture and documentaries, enabling viewers to intimately connect with local communities. ↩ While Mitch initially planned a six-week expedition, his path changed when a fellow traveler suggested he visit colonial Antigua, Guatemala. The town left a profound impact on him that altered the course of his entire life. He returned to the United States, but soon after made a decision: he would relocate to Guatemala for a year. Four decades later, he remains there, having built an amazing life around textiles and as an active participant in the local community. ↩ When he first arrived, Mitch faced the need to supplement his income. A friend of his from the U.S. presented an opportunity: to have him ship back any interesting items he found from Guatemala, to sell in and around New York. Riding his motorcycle to the highlands, Mitch discovered skilled weavers in the town of Momostenango who crafted exquisite wool rugs. Collaborating with the weavers, they developed new designs for the rugs and began exporting them. Mitch handled every aspect of the business, from creation to shipment, even meticulously removing twigs from the rough, hand-spooled and hand-dyed wool. ↩ As Mitch's business flourished, his friend Martha Bartlett played a pivotal role by introducing him to homeowners whose residences had been designed by influential figures, including favorites like Billy Baldwin and Albert Hadley. Mitch's aspirations quickly expanded to reproducing historical fabrics that these high-end designers could incorporate into international projects. When the trip to Momostenango became perilous due to internal conflicts (Guatemala's civil war lasted almost forty years) he invested in a loom to facilitate local production in Antigua. ↩ Over time, Mitch has cultivated an impressive factory. Now boasting over forty looms and a dedicated team of 250 employees, he has created a not only a thriving company, but a nurturing family. Women and men who work in the factory have honed skills and learned new techniques that build upon traditional backstrap and pedal looms and ikat techniques. ↩ Collaborating with Mitch, we have experienced the joy of crafting rugs, tapestries, wall fabrics, and throws. The intricate interplay of color, material, and weaving techniques in his creations is both inspiring and complex. Mitch, ever accommodating, has never shied away from our requests, consistently finding innovative solutions to bring them to fruition. We feel lucky to develop new designs for projects that are not only going to be unique and deeply personal, but will also aid in carrying on a tradition in local craft. ↩ To give back to the local community, Mitch and his talented daughter Jamie have created the only noncommercial space for exhibiting contemporary art in Guatemala. It is a difficult endeavor in a country with little philanthropy, yet they have managed to turn part of the factory into an exhibition space celebrating the work of local and foreign artists.

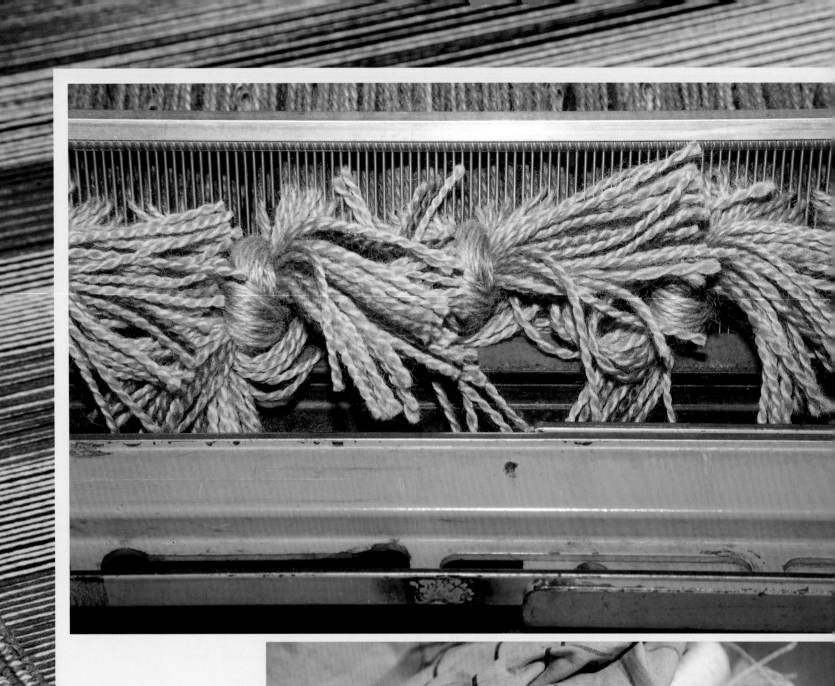

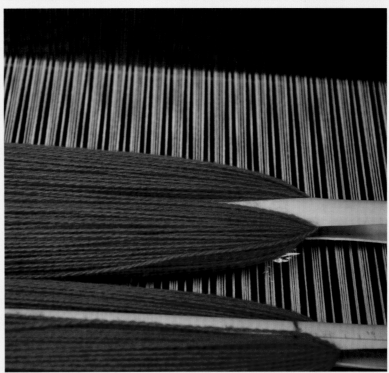
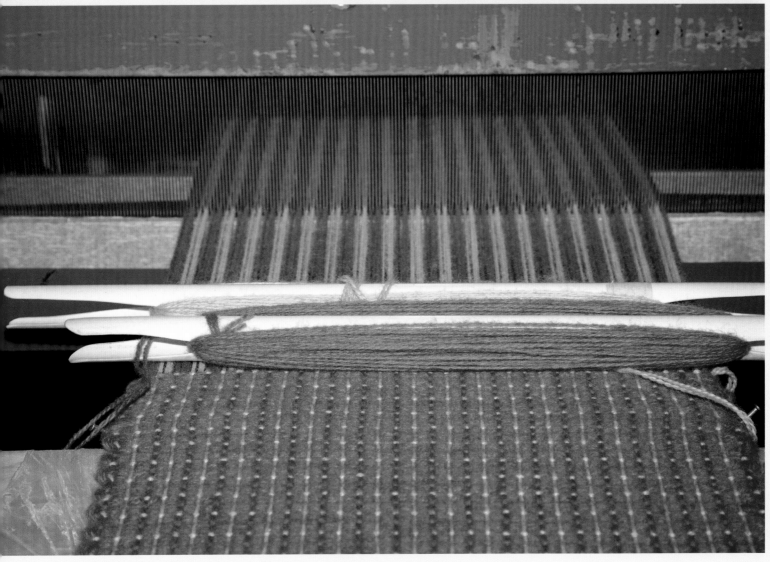

MITCHELL DENBURG ⊢ ANTIGUA, GUATEMA

A Lisa Eisner rodeo photo surveys a sitting room with walls covered in indigo burlap.

warwick avenue

↦ LONDON

In 2004, Rudy and I moved to London after I'd been offered a position running an auction house, a phenomenal chance to live, for the time, in the heaving center of the global art market. We'd spent the previous five years in a modest West Hollywood bungalow whose courtyard I'd planted with olive trees, geraniums, and pelargoniums that I had collected with my grandmother. For months before the move, I commuted from L.A. and always tacked on a few extra days to look at flats. Though I kept reluctantly adding money to our real estate budget, I found that the apartments only seemed to get bigger and uglier in proportion to the prices. I was beginning to feel desperate when a friend introduced us to an acquaintance looking for a "lodger." I don't think I've ever responded so viscerally to a series of rooms as I did to that apartment on Warwick Avenue. I loved it so intensely that, on our first viewing with the landlady, I cried. She was British enough to be embarrassed at my outburst, and promptly discounted the rent. ↵ We returned to California feeling triumphant but also well aware that we couldn't just re-create the home we loved so much on the far side of the Atlantic. For one thing, color is essential to the way I think about space. I've been painting since I was a kid and, while studying fine arts in college, focused on conceptual work with watercolors. Color is different everywhere, thanks to atmosphere and latitude. Hues that look great under the intense Pacific sun may not work in London—not because of the stereotypical assumptions about California sunshine and London gloom, but because the angle and quality of the light, even the density of the air, changes radically from one place to another. In Los Angeles, light bounces off the gray, green, and purple hills, off the parched desert and the blue ocean. The sun shines with sharp, dry intensity. L.A. light eats up color; almost nothing is too bright. In London the moist, gray-blue atmosphere makes hot primary colors much too shocking. ↵ As the move got closer, I would bring fabric samples with me to London and visit the space at different times of day to see how the light changed as it passed over them. We had sofas and headboards made in our favorite Los Angeles workshop and covered the walls with an Indian-inspired block print from my dear friend Peter Dunham's fabric line. We edited our furniture collection to make room for local finds, and I shipped over rolls of my favorite indigo burlap to cover the walls of the sitting room. We didn't want the place to look English, necessarily, but we wanted it to look at home in England. ↵ We loved that apartment and continually added art, furniture, and objects. It was a living space, never static. Rudy found a classic Memphis table by Michele De Lucchi locally that we used in the dining room. On trips to Istanbul we gathered antique Bessarabian carpets and antique roller-printed cottons from Russia. We collect to remember our travels, to marvel at craftsmanship, to hold onto things that are, quite simply, too beautiful to leave without. We never set out to acquire, never buy a chair just because we know there is a corner that could use filling. It's a principle we try and transmit to our clients: bring stories home, not things. Interesting objects will always speak to each other. Figure out what it is you love and, more important, why.

A large cardboard sculpture by Florian Baudrexel adds a modern touch to the stair hall.

121   Works from Los Angeles artists Kristin Calabrese and Patrick Lakey welcome visitors.   warwick avenue ↦ LONDON

123   The quetzal is the national bird of Rudy's homeland, Guatemala, and one of the most difficult animals to preserve, so finding this antique mount felt like a good omen.

Mexico City–based artist Miguel Calderón has long been a favorite of ours.

These were my favorite sheets ever, navy eyelet-trimmed Schweitzer,
which they sadly stopped making.

Rudy collected call girl adverts from London telephone booths to decorate our dressing room. The portrait is a Polaroid by Todd Eberle.

129

Leanne Shapton is truly the multi-hyphenate of multi-hyphenates, a term that only should be applied to people who have truly mastered multiple skills. Leanne is a talented writer, painter, editor, art director, graphic novelist, and swimmer. The Canadian wunderkind is based in New York City and has contributed to publications like *Maclean's* and the *National Post* as well as the *New York Times* and the *New York Review of Books*. She is articulate, urbane, and her books tell stories in unusual ways. But what gets *us* really excited are her paintings. ↵ Watercolor is considered by many to be one of the most difficult painting mediums to really master though it is often seen as a hobby—it is delicate, ephemeral, and relatively unforgiving. Rodman, who paints as well, became an instant fan of her loose, lyrical brushwork that often plays off the negative space of the unpainted paper. She exhibits a real confidence in the medium, creating pieces filled with humor, humanity, and vitality. She also has an excellent and unusual sense of color. ↵ Often, we follow an artist for years—pinning gallery invites to our corkboards, tearing pages out of magazines—before we get the chance to collaborate on a project together. Such was the case with Leanne; it wasn't until a fated coincidence in a beloved, though now closed, New York City restaurant that we finally connected. Rodman's first collaboration with Leanne was in 2017 when he commissioned her to develop the fair identity for Design Miami in 2017 after "mood boarding" a number of her illustrations and book covers and having been gifted her amazing book *Important Artifacts and Personal Property from the Collection of Lenore Doolan and Harold Morris, Including Books, Street Fashion, and Jewelry*, a love story told through a fictional auction catalog. ↵ We started discussing textile projects shortly after the Design Miami commission but nothing came to fruition until we realized had a shared passion for quilts. Leanne designed several quilts incorporating watercolors of patterns she designed that we printed on various textile bases for her, from velvet to a rough cotton/linen blend. Then we had them sewn together at her direction by a collective of women quilters in Mexico City. Leanne wanted to create an elevated version of those ubiquitous moving blankets—even utilizing that recognizable zigzag pattern we've all seen wrapped around furniture in U-Hauls. They were beautiful, idiosyncratic, and unexpected.

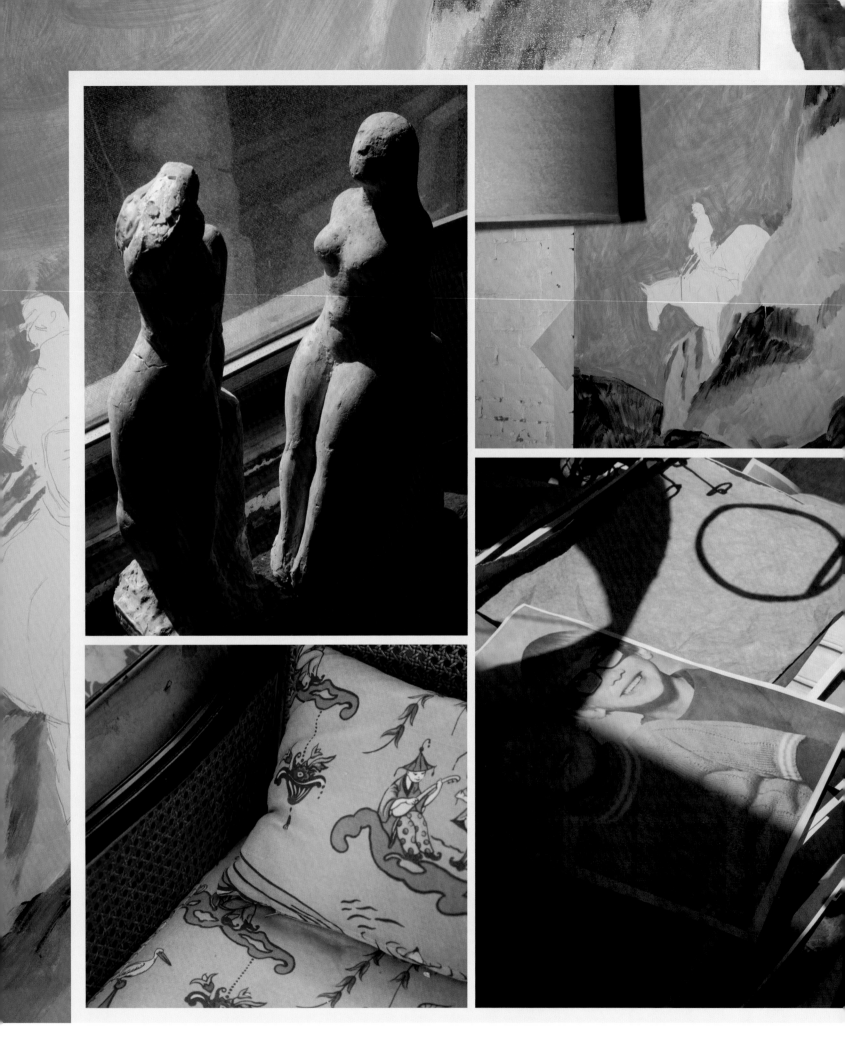

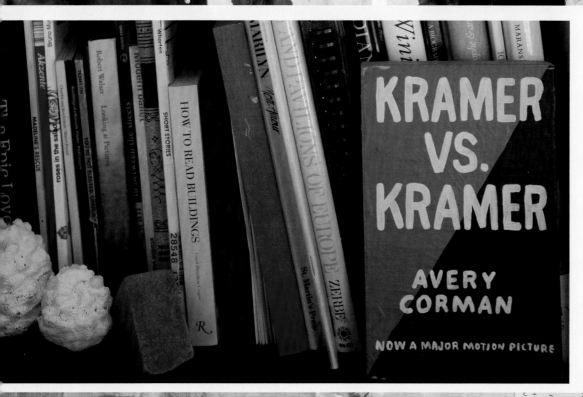

LEANNE SHAPTON ⇢ NYC

cherokee triangle

↦ KENTUCKY

Louisville is a small city placed at the lush green junction of the Midwest and the South, where the mighty Ohio River measures a mile across and the Kentucky Derby is proudly run the first weekend each May. It is a pretty, charming, definitively American town populated by warm, welcoming characters. Over the course of almost forty years, beginning in 1891, the great Frederick Law Olmsted and his firm designed seventeen individual parks connected by six parkways here—the largest of four such urban park systems created by the father of American landscape design—including the undulant sweep of Cherokee Park. ↩ A century ago, when the park was young, it sat near the city's eastern limits in a posh suburb of leafy streets and graceful homes. A little over a decade ago, I was invited to work on one of these historic houses and was immediately besotted with its idiosyncratic, almost mannerist, proportions: tall and slender and half hidden by towering old trees. It reminded me of the Victorian Gothic Addams Family compound or the sinister playfulness of Edward Gorey, at once quaint and a bit spooky. The clients, who would soon become intimate friends and with whom I would later collaborate on two other projects, had already lived in the house for many years. They knew what worked well and what didn't and wanted to update the space to better reflect their needs—and their personalities. ↩ The moment I'm invited to work on a new project, I set out to learn as much about its setting as I can. I am a born flâneur, so this process often involves long strolls through surrounding streets, allowing me to absorb the character of a neighborhood, district, or city. I can't understate the importance of looking beyond a project's immediate four walls. A sense of place—history, atmosphere, all the things that come together to make that ineffable thing we call "culture"—helps to create a kind of scaffolding that supports a project as it grows. Sometimes, however, as the project takes on a life of its own, that structure will buckle, splinter, and break.

Those are the moments that excite me most. I'm no historicist, so, as much as I love house museums, those marvelous windows into someone else's past, I can't imagine wanting to actually live in a period piece, hamstrung by the strictures of what was or was not strictly "accurate" for a given era. ↩ I am a firm adherent to the notion of Accidentism, first described in a 1958 manifesto of the same name written by the Austrian-Swedish designer Josef Frank toward the end of his successful career in architecture and design. Rejecting the tedium imposed by the development of an international "style," Frank wrote that "we should design our surroundings as if they originated by chance." It's an idea that manifests itself constantly in our work, particularly in contexts where objects and choices end up making a strange kind of sense precisely because they don't. At Cherokee Road, for instance, a pair Madeleine Castaing–inspired banquettes flank a Delft-tiled hearth, their cushions studded with hundreds of button tufts upholstered in a camouflage fabric that breaks the room's inherent pull toward formality. Clustered seating areas feature a nineteenth-century Swedish sofa, Italian rattan chairs from the 1950s, a pair of Jean Royère Petit Oeuf chairs, a Carlo Bugatti cabinet made the same year the house was built, and a violet cast-aluminum mirror from the contemporary American designer Misha Kahn. But somehow, it's not nearly as discordant as it sounds. ↩ These improbable juxtapositions reflect, at least to my mind, the warm and vibrant social world of a city populated by people from many walks of life. It's an approach to the idea of creating a vernacular that looks beyond navel-gazing materiality and form and addresses instead the spirit of a place, which is always defined by the people who live there. Today, bright colors peer through the windows of that forbidding façade, a wink and a welcome to draw visitors in. Old houses need fresh ideas. Sometimes those emanate from history, but historic properties must evolve, reflect authentic contemporary lives lived within. Because what else, in the end, is a house for?

The dining room serves as a gallery for beautiful objects including, left to right, a Kiki Smith sculpture,
Shiro Kuramata Acrylic stool, and a Studio Wieki Somers blown-glass amphora.

And what, for example, am I now seeing

A large Gert and Uwe Tobias piece greets visitors on their way to the kitchen. cherokee triangle ↦ KENTUCKY

A dress captured by Malian photographer Seydou Keïta inspired the hand-screened striped silk curtains in the Sitting Room.

Rodman made cast bronze Apple Branch lanterns with his old friend
Jan Cox for the main hall.

Louisville-based architect Thomas Kute refashioned the kitchen porch
into an airy breakfast room and study.

The graphic floor is made of old-fashioned linoleum; it's just arranged so that its pattern appears to have "slipped" in a modern way.

John Fowler inspired the curtains made of custom Prelle silks woven in three shades.

David Wiseman made a custom terrazzo-and-bronze buffet table to fit the room, and Thaddeus Wolfe crafted the iceberg-like glass-and-bronze sconces.

cherokee triangle ↦ KENTUCKY

A sleeping porch was refashioned into a perfect tree-shaded workroom.

Art rotates frequently throughout the house; here a large painted piece on paper by Abraham Cruzvillegas adds a jolt of color to the sitting room.

Marco Rountree Cruz has been a cultural agitator since his teenage years. Artist, muralist, gallerist, and curator—he flows between these professions seamlessly. He is a self-taught artist who started his practice by deeply enmeshing himself in the art scene in Mexico City in the early 2000s. His current work is informed by his insider access; he looks at art for art's sake and acts as a refracting mirror of sorts for modern interpretations of art history. He has a light and critical touch, and he often uses humor as a tool to draw in the observer. In Marco's practice, objects, surfaces, and images can appear in nontraditional contexts and coinhabit unexpected environments. His work establishes a conversation with other artists, creators, and makers, often across time, meaning his work might include pre-Columbian artifacts, or everyday objects like books and the work of fellow artists. ↵ We met Marco while he was doing a short residency in England. It was a loose program that allowed him to do research, conceptualize projects, and come up with his own interpretation for output. For example, one of the works he created there entailed planting a small tree inside the trunk of a dead tree, then documenting what happened. It was a light, conscious, and thoughtful intervention that really spoke to us. We have also been drawn to his large-scale works for a long time. Marco makes murals featuring bold graphics, animals, and characters—a reference to the Mexican Muralism movement of the twentieth century, but using a wide gamut of materials. He can quickly cover walls with blue painter's tape or collect *tezontle* (volcanic rock) pebbles in black and red and diligently glue them to a surface. He creates environments that are full of art history references but usually have a through line of invented narratives. ↵ Marco has now partnered with two other artists to start a gallery with locations in Mexico City and Guadalajara. They are artist-run spaces that focus on giving shows to emerging artists to jump-start their careers. Their group shows usually draw from artists working in both cities. They take chances and give voice to talented artists outside of the established gallery circuit. Marco's position as a longtime art world insider/outsider gives him a unique viewpoint to understanding what's new and innovative. He is connected to a younger generation of artists and his events are always thrumming with young creatives. ↵ For the Louisville project featured here, we approached Marco to come up with a proposal for a large mural that would be visible from the front hall. It is a transitional space, where the landing of the stairs converges with the doors leading to the kitchen and informal dining room. The piece needed to be bold and have a presence, but it could not overwhelm the entire room or the other art cohabiting in the space. Over the span of two weeks, climbing on ladders and improvised scaffolding, Marco worked with black painter's tape to create a mural of cranes and lilies that obliquely evokes a seventeenth-century Japanese screen painting.

A huge vintage Indian dhurrie found in Santa Fe was refashioned to fit the oval sitting room. Art by Marilyn Minter hangs above the fireplace.

san marino island

↦ MIAMI

Rudy moved to Miami for the first time in 2000; I was still in New York, though I commuted down as often as I could. In 2012, Rudy's work took us back and, shortly after we arrived, he found an extraordinary 1930s bungalow on a quiet island in Biscayne Bay, just a few bridges away from Miami Beach. The house was as strange as could be. I reacted as viscerally to it as I had to the flat in London—this place inspired tears, too, but not of happiness. Mostly my displeasure was due to its putrid stench. More than thirty cats had lived with the sickly hoarder/owner who'd preceded us. Still, beneath the piles of boxes overflowing with yellowing newspapers, Rudy and I saw an idiosyncratic gem. Its bedrooms and bathrooms radiated like spokes from a central hub of an oval great room. The layout was bizarre —anomalous enough, really, that I still have a hard time picturing it in my mind— but I firmly believe that the best design comes from working within imposed limits rather than forcing a space to try and accommodate creature comforts that you can almost certainly live without. ↵ Taking the surrounding houses of a similar vintage as our guide, Rudy and I set to work restoring that odd, endearing building to a more charming state. You always lose something by stripping everything away and starting over, since what begins as an attempt to

"improve" can too easily denude a house of whatever made is special in the first place. I would rather sacrifice high-tech kitchen appliances and closet space than the original animating spirit. ↵ Rudy and I both adored working on this project, though it should be noted that I tend to suffer (or benefit?) from project amnesia; I forget (or repress?) the dramas of city permits, absentee work crews, and inevitable delays. Light, climate, heat, and, perhaps above all, the local vernacular are all radically different in South Florida than they are in any other place we've lived, so we took the project as an opportunity to immerse ourselves in an entirely new design language. The southernmost metropolis in the U.S., Miami is where the Deep South meets the Caribbean. It is also, fundamentally, a city shaped by migration and a rich variety of influences. Spanish Colonial mansions live side by side with Bahamian cottages and an exuberant, maximalist modernism. The city is filled with handmade hydraulic cement tiles, often referred to as "Cuban tiles," used widely across the West Indies, and also poured terrazzo floors—an idiomatic part of global modernism—plus the streamlined curves and porthole windows that are hallmarks of European Art Deco— a style that permeated Latin America in the early twentieth century. It is so clearly a place built for pleasure. Its architecture—eccentric, contrived, gloriously campy—seems designed to inspire glamour and intrigue. Our house in Miami was designed to celebrate and exalt all those elements. A decorative language, to us, feels not just natural here, but inevitable.

An Erika Verzutti bronze peacock sculpture watches over the dining room.

Old school chairs, a vintage Michele De Lucchi table, and a Jonas Wood pastel leaning against the curved wall each inject an unexpected, bright color to this vibrant room.

Luis González Palma's photograph gazes peacefully over a vintage
Danish tambour cabinet.

The local chef supply store made our stainless steel open shelves
and super-deep sinks.

The collaged watercolor work by Colombian artist Gabriel Silva Rubio
was one of Rudy's first auction buys.

Renowned German toymaker Renate Müller made the hippo ottoman at my request.

indian bean

↦ KENTUCKY

Indian Bean is a nonworking farm in rural Kentucky, surrounded by tobacco fields and studded with copses of high-domed catalpa trees that lend the property its name. It's not an especially fancy part of the Kentucky countryside—it's free of hats and horses and high-stakes socializing. That's why our clients—a surprising, thoughtful, deeply engaged couple with whom we've worked with on three houses now—fell in love with it. By the time we started work at the farm, we'd been collaborating for some years on the family's house in Louisville, developing a rapport and mutual trust in one another's interests and perspectives. Our close, almost filial bond allowed us to develop a shorthand through which we could experiment and explore together. We already knew very well what kind of pillows they liked, for instance, exactly the sort of basic but essential detail you learn the first time you work with someone. Here, we could make bigger moves, take bigger risks, build bigger dreams. ↵ If memory serves, I actually visited Indian Bean long before we started working on the project together. On my first visit to Kentucky to meet the clients, before I even saw the Louisville house that I would eventually be hired to redesign, they brought me out to this very farm, which they've owned since the late 1990s. It was an unusual "interview," if you can even call it that—more like an opportunity to feel out our compatibility, a chance to start our relationship with a friendship rather than a transaction. All to say, I knew the property well when I started working on it, and was familiar with the changes the family had made over the years—like the former feedlot they'd turned into a generous kitchen garden anchored by corrugated-metal sheds, natural cabanas for the nearby swimming pool. ↵ One of the first significant interventions we made together was inviting the American artist Roy McMakin to collaborate. Pulling an artist into the mix is, from my point of view, less about achieving a specific end and more about inviting new ideas and inspirations. Roy in particular brings an inimitable combination of earnestness and irony, of sincere transparency and mischievous subterfuge. As we walked around the property—the farm, garden, barn, and house—Roy, in a stroke of genius, suggested that we create an outdoor dining room just off the kitchen. No walls, no roof, just a table and chairs with maybe a breakfront for a buffet and to display buckets of freshly cut flowers. Far more than a covered patio or a table under a gazebo ever could, this space connects to the landscape. The deck, level with the clipped grass, feels like a picnic blanket thrown across the lawn. Chickens cluck happily at our feet. Eggs taste fresher here. ↵ There are moments like this throughout Indian Bean, moments of deep humor and wit, narratives that we invented together to lend texture and weight to our decisions. Classic pieces of Italian modernism that we scattered throughout the project became, in our imaginations, family heirlooms inherited from a Turin-born stepfather whose taste in design lasted longer in the family than he had. The idea started as a joke, but it ultimately became a real justification for our outré choice to install a vintage Tawayara Boxing Ring by Masanori Umeda—a rare and iconic work of early Memphis design—in a Kentucky barn, right next to a wood-burning fireplace with expansive views over rolling fields. There is a measure of folly and delight in that room. It is also an undeniably cozy spot to read a book or talk for hours with friends. Design is not about perfection—at least not for us. It's about engagement and pleasure, which is another way to say relationships. ↵ It's rare to find clients who are interested in working toward something more than curating a highly "correct" but utterly spiritless cluster of handsome rooms. Speeding past the received rules of "good taste" has allowed us to rush headlong into deeper emotional and aesthetic territory. Adherence to tradition may be the most direct route to familiarity—you're sure to recognize a room, after all, if you've seen it many times before—but it's certainly not the only one.

Mixmatched Ankara cotton batik fabrics paper the library.

indian bean ↦ KENTUCKY

A favorite Josef Frank cotton print is used to bold advantage on the chairs;
the rug is a huge custom salvaged nylon fishing rope made in Maine.

indian bean ↦ KENTU

Every bedroom is a mix of cozy patterns and prints.   indian bean ⇥ KENTUCKY

Masanori Umeda's iconic Tawaraya boxing ring conversation pit from 1981 anchors the barn.

Louisville-based Monica C. Mahoney refashioned the pool table into a work of art.   **indian bean** ↦ KENTUCKY

Roy McMakin conceived the pool shed shower room.

indian bean ↦ KENTUCKY

We have been regular customers of Chiarastella Cattana since she opened her first shop in Venice in 2004, and luckily over the years we have become collaborators and friends. Her eye is unparalleled, her textiles exquisite, her desire to keep traditions alive singular. Walking through the large glass door of her shop is transporting—you enter a zone of aesthetic gentleness that immediately instills calm and a sense of well-being. ↵ For centuries now Venice, and the Veneto region, has been one of the most generative places on the planet for art, architecture, and craft. Its glass is perhaps the most famous medium, but it also continues to foster lace-making, mosaics, goldsmithing, weaving, and carving. Chiarastella is a keeper of knowledge about how to create high-quality textile goods for the home. She works with all kinds of makers to realize her designs—she refers for example to "the old man" who has a special loom in the Sud Tyrol mountains for special jacquards, and says no one knows how to use it except him, meaning the technique will sadly die when he does. Her work contains elements of both design and detective work—it's both physical and anthropological, since she travels around Italy searching for people to make her goods on pedal or shuttle looms, often finding the last craftspeople in certain specialties as younger generations have lost the interest or knowledge to make traditional products or work specific machines. So, her work becomes a kind of cherished living record of vanishing techniques and know-how. ↵ Stella, as she is known

to friends, is not native to Venice, but arrived in the lagoon city from Milan, where she had worked in fashion and textiles, following the father of her daughter, who was very much a local. She started designing home textiles in 2001 and has quietly grown her collection year after year. Sometimes it takes an outsider to press for innovation in an established industry or to reinvigorate a local craft, to be inspired by what has become considered passé or simply old-fashioned. Stella consistently designs and makes the most beautiful woven fabrics, working in sustainable fibers including cotton, linen, wool, and cashmere to create blankets, shawls, napkins, towels, and tablecloths. She also makes sturdier fabrics for upholstery and now has several coordinated collections of textiles by the yard. She worked with RP Miller over the course of a year to develop a custom heavier-weight linen stripe for a sofa, tinkering with it through multiple variations until it was just right. Nothing Stella makes is anonymously manufactured; her fabrics are made by her cadre of craftspeople, and the presence of the human hand is visible and tactile in everything she makes. Her attention to detail is unmatched as well as her eye for color. Swatches of her textiles, folded tea towels, and corners of throws frequently figure into the early ideation of our collaborative projects because they capture all that we love and value. Tone, texture, harmony, and the unexpected—it's all there.

Birds show up in many forms in all our homes; this one features
a white Jeffry Mitchell ceramic falcon and a taxidermied peacock.

ninth street

When Rudy and I met twenty-five years ago, we both lived on 76th Street, me on the east side and Rudy on the west. We were both working our first jobs, me at Christie's, Rudy at a commodities trading firm. My place was tiny and grim, as first New York apartments tend to be. Rudy lived on the third floor of an Upper West Side brownstone overlooking a row of mature plane trees. But what really caught my eye in that space was a sprawling 1994 painting by Gabriel Silva Rubio hanging in the living room: a collection of yellowed pages, like a deconstructed sketchbook, painted over with watercolor figures that resemble sea creatures and nymphs. I knew right then that we were wired similarly, excited by the same things. ↩ Since those first New York Apartments we've lived in Los Angeles and London, Miami and Guatemala City, Boston, Mexico City, and, more than once, Manhattan, where we're still based half of the time today. We returned to New York from London in 2010 after almost a decade away. Coming back to New York, we knew we wanted to be in Greenwich Village. This place—the first we rented together in the city—was imperfectly perfect. High ceilings, big windows . . . and probably a quarter of the size of our flat in London. That meant moving many beloved possessions into storage, where they awaited uncertain fates. Editing your furnishings requires a lot of clarity about what it is you really need. In New York, we built serviceable bookshelves and lots of storage. It's so easy to get caught up in what the media or, worse still, other people tell us to want, but design isn't didactic. It's experiential. ↩ When I look at photos of this apartment, it's abundantly clear that I wasn't quite ready to give up Warwick Avenue in London, at least not the spirit of the place. I've always been nostalgic, and pieces of London stayed with us here on 9th street, though the new apartment couldn't accommodate a fraction of the usual number of guests we'd been used to hosting—or a fraction of our books. Preserving the spirit of our previous house, though, quickly allowed us to feel deeply at home again. We shared space with the things we'd collected abroad, each a mnemonic vessel for a story or experience. We made space for the stuffed peacock we'd found at Deyrolle in Paris, the tiled Roger Capron coffee table from a dealer on the Pimlico Road, and an unusual Martino Gamper piece made from recycled Lutrario Ballroom chairs by Carlo Molino. New York, the place we met, remains our anchor, the gravitational center of our peripatetic lives, so it maybe makes sense that this home would become—to use an old cliché—a melting pot, a place where our many worlds could come together.

Rudy has been a lover of photography forever; this Nan Goldin was a family gift.

Rodman has loved American quilts since childhood, and has collected and used them in projects from his first.

This Rick Owens chair was a special commission, and lead to a multi-year collaboration with the designer.

Martin Gamper is a designer we have long admired. This chair by him was made from upcycled vintage Lutrario Ballroom chairs by Carlo Mollino. An RP Miller textiles linen curtain conceals storage with dainty pattern.

truro

↦ CAPE COD

The Outer Cape of Massachusetts—that slender hook of land that bends north to separate the Atlantic from Cape Cod Bay—has been drawing creatives of one kind or another for almost a century, if not longer. Starting in the late 1930s, some of the most interesting minds in America built summer houses, painting studios, and beach shacks here, dotted amid scrubby oaks and pitch pines, down sandy tracks that wound between kettle ponds formed by retreating ice sheets some 18,000 years ago. The Hungarian-German architect Marcel Breuer built his summer home here, followed by painter James Lechay and the Russian-born British writer, industrial designer, architect, and academic Serge Chermayeff. Florence and Hans Knoll, the Saarinens, and Walter Gropius all rented houses here through the years—a latter-day Bauhaus on the Beach. ↩ Perhaps the best known local figure was the architect Hayden Walling, whose present-day fame rests largely on two houses: the Halprin House and Studio, its simple frame of two-by-fours filled with floor-to-ceiling glass, and the project he built for Lechay, with its raked roofline and angled outer wall. Iconic projects both. So you can imagine my delight when our clients from Kentucky managed to acquire the home that Walling built for himself in the late 1930s and called us. With its steep gables and clapboard siding, the house predates the architect's shift toward a more hard-lined modernism. All houses speak if we listen, and this one demanded that we tread lightly so as not to destroy its unusual, transitional spirit. ↩ Of course, the program needed to change in some fundamental ways to accommodate the needs of the family. Children were transitioning into young adulthood, so the parents were beginning to think of adapting to as-yet-unknown futures: jobs, partners, children. We brought on the New York–based architect Malachi Connolly, also an advisor to the Cape Cod Modern House Trust. His years of experience working in the area gave him direct access to many of the region's best modern houses for inspiration, including Walling's. Working with Malachi, we designed a new guest house, sited away from the original structure but close enough to be integrated into the shared life of the building. And while the family's homes in Kentucky leaned into their more eclectic tendencies, here on the Cape, with a heritage of Pilgrim austerity and that rich and rigorous intellectual history, we made rooms that would feel neither old nor new, just simple and natural. These would be spaces for sandy feet and hastily made beds and kitchen sinks stacked with lunch dishes left behind because the beach suddenly called. That's the kind of house it wanted to be. ↩ To me, a summer house is ruined the moment it feels winterized, robbed of that gleeful sense of a fleeting, weightless season. Of course, houses do need to withstand extremes in weather—the trick is making them feel as if they might not. To strike that balance, we chose homasote across the project, a cellulose fiberboard used widely since the 1920s. Walling had used it originally as well. Richly textured and humble, with a fantastic ability to absorb sound, it seemed essential to the house's easy, no-fuss energy. The furniture throughout—armchairs by Charlotte Perriand and Eero Saarinen, a rare standing lamp by Ettore Sottsass, an original FJ-55 chair by Finn Juhl—gestures toward Walling's future turn toward high modernism without (I hope!) falling into the trap of looking like a fetishistic mod-style film set. To achieve that meant repurposing what was already there, resisting the urge to "fix" things and, instead, leaving traces of what came before. That's the challenge and the joy of a project like this: creating a sense of history inside the house that can match the real history of its bones, the sense of a life built gradually over the course of a half century. It's not just preparing for the future, it's also caring for the past.

An old wooden table was painted to connect in high style with the Michele De Lucchi side table.

There is truly no substitute for collecting over the years; here pieces including vintage
Eero Saarinen Womb Chairs mix seamlessly with recent editions like the yellow camelback sofa.

truro ⇾ CAPE COD

In this cozy spot to read or catch up on work, a vintage Andrea Branzi Memphis Sofa
peeks into view.

truro ↦ CAPE COD

Vintage Scandinavian pieces mix with contemporary objects well, like the Fabien Cappello hanging pendant.

The walls are covered in craft paper, decorated with hand-painted chalk stripes.

199   RP Miller was inspired by a fragment of vintage paper to reincarnate its pattern as grasscloth wallpaper.

Rudy designed the steel side tables with colored acrylic inserts.

The water tower creates a truly reclusive, perfect reading/napping spot.

We have been collectors all our lives, and the drive to gather informs every aspect of our practice and way of living. We love to find and discover new, unexpected things. We don't honestly remember how we first connected with the Los Angeles–based Ryan Belli the first time, but we are certain we were instantly struck by his beautifully executed, thoughtful, often joyous design work. Our friends Monica and Jill at Site Unseen had him on their "hot list" in 2019, but we know we had seen some of his work before then. In any case, once he hit our radar, we knew we wanted to find a way to collaborate with him. Rodman went to visit his studio and was enthralled by the work and the designer making it. ↩ Although Ryan is originally from upstate New York, he and his work seem to exude an authentic air of California—a definite compliment from our perspective—independent and full of spirit. Ryan is unfettered by expectations or traditions and follows his own sources of inspiration. Often working in hand-carved wood in his Pasadena studio, a sense of humor and lightness pervades all his output. Forms look soft and malleable, even in oak. We have said before that his language is what would have happened if the Flintstones had commissioned Jean Royère—they would have ended up with sofas by Ryan. There is a solidness and weight, yet the work never feels ponderous or pretentious. He has a deft hand at combining color, understanding that color has both weight and volume, and he plays equally well with texture and materiality. We are delighted by design that defies conventions or expectations, and Ryan's work does this effortlessly—but never carelessly. Sometimes making an object that exudes a sense of carefree freedom, a nonchalance, is decidedly much more work than creating one that relies on rigidity and sturdy forms, which usually winds up feeling weighed down with self-conscious seriousness. ↩ Certainly, some of this attractive irreverence may have seeped into Ryan during his years working in the studio of our old friends Simon and Nikki Haas, two of the most recognized contemporary designers of our generation. Their sense of humor and interest in fantasy is perhaps even more pronounced than Ryan's. He worked on special projects for the Haas Brothers and his commitment to craft and material qualities was undoubtedly honed there. Since starting his own practice, Ryan has been consistently building a body of work that is singular in its inventiveness and commitment to handcrafted works, and we expect to continue collaborating with him for many years to come.

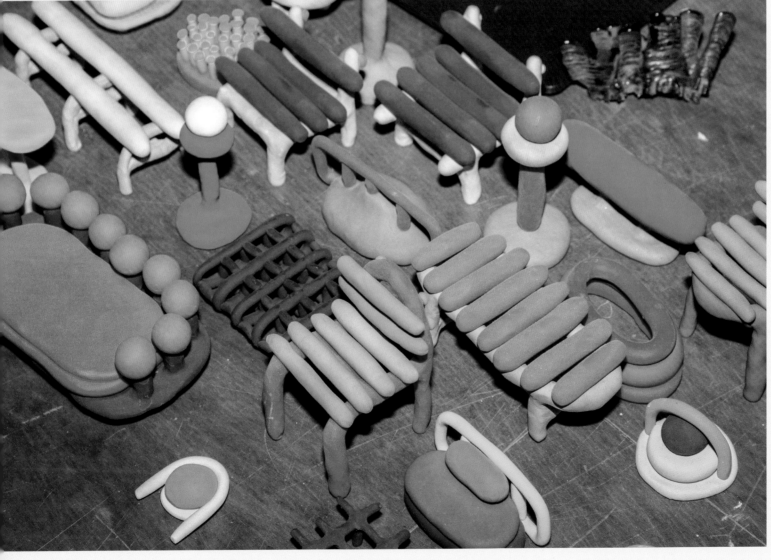

RYAN BELLI ↦ LOS ANGELES

Vintage Afra & Tobia Scarpa Soriana Chairs from Rudy's grandparents' home in Guatemala and a painting by Donna Huanca bring color and dimension to the living room.

palmas

↦ MEXICO

New York remains as dear to us as ever, but we now spend about half our time in Mexico City, and that migration has always felt like destiny. Mexico is such a powerful cultural force for Californians as well as Guatemalans; both our families have long-standing ties to the city, so it's always loomed large in our imaginations. Both of us also had close friends at college who hailed from Mexico's immense capital—Rudy and I studied on opposite coasts, but those friends, as luck would have it, knew each other—and we've both been engaged with work here for over two decades. So, after years of talking about it and while sitting in a taxi one afternoon in 2018, we finally decided to up and move. Within hours we'd confirmed an available space for the gallery we wanted to open and, just as important, had an apartment to live in.   ↩   I'd had my eye on this building for years: a radical modernist apartment block built by the midcentury master Augusto Álvarez between 1948 and 1952, just a few years before he designed the Torre Latinoamericana, still one of the city's most iconic landmarks. In our building and its twin next door, slender steel pilasters slip past horizontal bands of glass, traversing delicate concrete slabs and meeting the ground as pilotis: an impeccable, early example of the Miesian International Style in Mexico. It was also a relatively early expression of high-rise architecture in this seismically active metropolis and the first apartment building in the swish surrounding neighborhood of Lomas de Chapultepec. It seems to float over its generous garden, and tree branches brush the eighth-floor windows of our bedroom.   ↩   Though we considered the layout of the apartment perfect, the previous owners had installed popcorn ceilings and ugly wooden floors in an unnatural shade of orange. We set about restoring what we loved—the oak paneling and cabinets in the sitting room and the densely patterned tile in the kitchen— and painting over what we didn't, like the kitchen cabinets that had been stained an overbearing faux mahogany. We hate waste and always look for ways to conserve what we can, so paint is one of our preferred tricks of the trade.   ↩   In the bathrooms, we pulled out oppressive veined stone that clad every flat surface and replaced it with handmade square tiles: black on the floor, pale pink on the walls, inspired by the superlative kitchen at Luis Barragán's Casa Prieto López. Blocks of color—namely chalkboard-green floors throughout the apartment, a canary-yellow kitchen, and a cactus-green study—help define and organize the space, making it feel bigger than its actual square footage. Although we brought a few important pieces from Guatemala, particularly a suite of Afra chairs and ottomans, most of the furniture was made new in collaboration with designers represented by the gallery, including young talents Pedro y Juana, Fabien Cappello, Agnes Studio, and Lanza Atelier. We imagined the apartment as an evolving, habitable showroom, a space to showcase the artistry that enticed us here in the first place. Like all our houses, we aim to make the Mexico City apartment a celebration—of color, place, and chance, but also of the many years and experiences that led us here.

From left to right, a neon sculpture by Gabriel Rico, a textile wall piece by Jason Yates, and a painted metal pendant by Pedro y Juana add artistic drama to the dining room.

May You Live In Interesting Times

BIENNALE ARTE 2019 EXHIBITION

PARTICIPATING COUNTRIES & COLLATERAL EVENTS

Blue chairbacks that notch into the Dinner at Eight Table by Lanza Atelier with
Adam Silverman hold an ongoing conversation with an indigo-glazed ceramic orb.

Fabien Cappello's Silla Tropical chairs, an Ana Segovia painting, a Piovenefabi standing lamp, and custom rug by Agnes Studio all relate in a texture-rich living room.

A Sam Falls painting fits well among the office's bookshelves.   palmas ↦ MEXICO

A Pedro Reyes volcanic stone table, RP Miller's Peter's Stripe fabric on the wall, and an RP Miller Sturbridge bedcover infuse this bedroom with calming linear rationality.

A Fabien Cappello Fruit Lamp and a Hongos brass mirror by Anndra Neen add unexpected
color and form to a tiled bath.

We suspect the kitchen tiles may be original to the building;
we paired them with Fabien Cappello colored glass pendant lights.

A Fernando Laposse loofah screen and Gaetano Pesce x Raf Simons special edition Feltri Chair create sculpture from everyday bedroom items.

palmas ↦ MEXICO

Fabien Cappello is a French designer who has been living and working in Mexico since 2016. From the day he founded his own studio, in London in 2010, Fabien has been focused on working with local makers and techniques in every design. It is not unusual for Fabien to see a technique, a material, or a craftsperson and feel an urgent need to collaborate immediately. Rather than designing a piece and then looking for a maker to execute his own vision, he frequently works in reverse—whether it's finding a new form where he can apply a hyper-local craft technique or drafting an innovative industrial production proposal. He is committed to designing for and with people, so there is community energy inherent in all he touches. ↵ Fabien has won numerous international awards, residencies, and recognitions, and has shown at the Musée de Arts Décoratifs in Paris, the Musée de Arts Décoratifs de Bordeaux, at the esteemed Villa Noailles, and the Denver Art Museum. Magazines have anointed him by placing him on hot lists and have lauded his use of color and innovative materials. He is internationally recognized within the contemporary design community in and outside Mexico as a rising star. We have been so pleased to work with him on many different projects. ↵ Four years after establishing his prolific studio in the dense and bustling historic heart of downtown Mexico City, Fabien was inspired to move to Guadalajara, where he had been teaching frequently at the university level. Guadalajara is one of Mexico's most interesting cities in terms of craft and art production, and Fabien's output has only benefitted with the access to additional makers. Since moving to Mexico, his work has been tied to the incredibly diverse and abundant material culture that is at the heart of the city's character. People in Mexico still make things by hand frequently, and often after having been taught a craft by a relative. Fabien exalts this important aspect of Mexican life and culture and collaborates closely with individual craftspeople to create his work. ↵ We are constantly working with Fabien in the development of pieces for his practice, and he has also designed numerous special pieces for our interiors projects. It's safe to say that since we started working with him, his works appear in some way in all our work. We cannot get enough of his exuberant mosaic tables and cabinets, his candy-colored glass lamps and pendants, his fiberglass planters and recent velvet-upholstered *butacas*. The world of Fabien is exuberant, yet there is such a clear through line of philosophy and aesthetic that is happy but serious and grounded.

hacienda los milagros

There's a particular built language that has come to dominate Mexican beach houses: geometric volumes with sprawling terraces shaded by thatched *palapas*. It's a graceful, sensible adaptation for the country's rugged coastline, and one that I am personally fond of. The Hacienda Los Milagros—a sprawling mansion built in the 1990s in the beach town of Punta Mita, up the coast from the city of Puerto Vallarta— had nothing to do with that style at all. Were it not for the crashing waves just outside, the building, with its stucco walls and heavy wooden ceiling beams, might seem more at home among the highlands of the Bajío in central Mexico, a region characterized by its colonial towns, ornate churches, and cattle ranches.   ↩ Our clients purchased this property from its original owners, the Texan philanthropist Anne Marion and her husband John, former chairman of Sotheby's. By the time they brought us on they'd already opened up the windows and doors to let in the spectacular Pacific light, pared down the original project's ornamental detailing, and streamlined its interior distribution. This allowed us to spend our first meeting focused not on the nuts and bolts of how they needed the house to work, but rather on dreaming up a story to guide our heavily collaborative design process. We decided that day that the house should feel like the property of a studio-era Hollywood director who'd fallen passionately in love with Mexico. It was a complete fantasy, of course—some houses demand a bit of whimsy—but it also framed the strong central value that shaped the project. We planned to source everything we could in Mexico.   ↩ Too many people today seek out a neutered, homogenized, globalized beige aesthetic, a bland "good taste" designed to please everyone. It's usually achieved through design choices that evoke absolutely no emotion whatsoever. I stand firmly against the notion of "good taste" because those who claim to have it, as far as I'm concerned, share a lack of interest, lack of curiosity, and an all-encompassing obsession with personal comfort and/or what other people think. I do, however, believe strongly in celebrating local taste, and few places speak to me more powerfully than Mexico's Pacific coast. For years, my grandparents would spend a few weeks each year playing cards, eating seafood, and visiting friends in Puerto Vallarta. I couldn't have been much older than twelve when, on one of my annual visits, I started my first collection of crafts and folk art, picked up at the tourist markets in Vallarta's old town. Even then I believed in the value of real things made by real people, the imperfections that come from the intervention of human hands over the manufactured perfection of mass-produced luxury goods. We all agreed that this house, for all its opulence and excess, should capture the same transporting power that those objects had for me in my childhood, a goal we would accomplish by showcasing contemporary Mexican art, craft, and design.   ↩ The Hacienda was an ideal canvas. We commissioned an elaborate ceramic tile mosaic from the artisan Ángel Santos. Formed, dried, painted, and fired over the course of months in Santos's studio in Tonalá, it depicted a pastoral landscape in keeping with the house's fantastical intent. The Mexico City–based designers Pedro y Juana produced laser-cut lamps from multicolored metal and hanging planters in a powdery, mineral pink for over the bar. We asked Marcela Calderón, whose ceramic studio Taller 36 draws on her family's long history in the craft town of Patamban, to make a series of ceramic platters that depict creatures from the ocean. We worked with painter Ana Segovia, a rising star in Mexico City's art scene, to produce a series of portraits of bullfighters. This spirit of making and turning to craftspeople to add depth carries through the entire project. I like to imagine that, when the owners paddle back from a world-class break just beyond their property line—they're avid surfers— they return to their home with a special sense of pride in knowing exactly where they are.

223   Rudy designed the hanging parrot lamps.

Marcella Calderón of Taller 36 was commissioned to make the hanging platters, and we translated Xian of the Death's tattoo elements into a bronze emblem for the house.

hacienda los milagros ↦ MEXICO

Hector Zamora created the terra-cotta installation in the main hall. hacienda los milagros ↦ MEX

Pedro y Juana, the Mexico City–based designers, made special hanging planters and lights for the bar.

hacienda los milagros ↦ MEXICO

Craftspeople from all over Mexico are responsible for the dining room's furniture, lighting and ceramics.

hacienda los milagros ⇥ MEXICO

Tanya Aguiñiga created this incredible wall hanging, and Agnes Studio the pair of hand-carved geometric coffee tables.

hacienda los milagros ↦ MEXICO

Upholstered walls dotted with symmetric hand-painted panels ensure great sound in the media room.

hacienda los milagros ↦

We designed custom "HLM" hooks, pulls, and various hardware and accessories used across the property.

Hand-painted tiles from Tonalá enliven the master bath's walls, while a HLM wicker stool made for the house adds contrasting texture.

hacienda los milagros ↦ MEXICO

We are continually on the lookout for artists, makers, designers, and creatives of all kinds to engage in collaborative projects. We enjoy proposing new ideas and occasionally suggesting ways to stretch someone's artistic practice, leading to diverse outputs within the same discipline. One such collaboration is exemplified in our partnership with Chris Castañeda, also known as Xian of the Death, for the Hacienda Los Milagros project in Mexico. ↵ Rudy has long been an avid admirer of tattoos, constantly exploring the work of tattoo artists to learn about various practices and styles. Though he boasts a few small tattoos, his aspirations always leaned toward collaborating with a tattoo artist on more extensive, substantial pieces. This desire led us to Chris Castañeda's profile on social media. As we delved into her artistic realm and learned about her work, a magical synergy unfolded; we began encountering friends, artists, and visitors to AGO who had adorned themselves with her creations. Chris's distinctive hand and inspiration seemed all around us. ↵ Chris, a graduate in visual arts from La Esmeralda, known as one of Mexico City's renowned art schools, initially envisioned a career in photography. After setting up a small studio to capture images, her journey took a transformative turn during a residency program in Iceland. There, she experienced an epiphany—she felt a lack of fulfillment and pride in her photographic endeavors, but heard a clear message to consider tattoo. This revelation prompted a shift, leading her to embrace the path of a tattoo artist; she dismantled her studio and bought a tattoo machine on a whim. ↵ Her fascination with magic, symbolism,

and the occult found expression in her drawings-turned-tattoos. Immersed in the goth/punk scene, Chris honed her skills through the support of her community, quickly earning a reputation for her special touch and profound, inspiring personal style. Her themes often revolve around the celebration of femininity, nature, and mythological forces. Constantly envisioning designs that seamlessly merge with the skin, she has now cultivated an artistic practice that extends beyond tattoo, with a cosmology of drawings and paintings serving as intriguing complements. ↵ Captivated by Chris's symbolism and the elegance of her artistry, we envisioned a unique project exploring the idea of tattooing a house—infusing a home with positive symbols and drawings that narrate a story. Collaborating with Chris, we came up with ideas to turn her drawings into three-dimensional facets of Milagros's interiors. This included a bronze sculpture at the home's entrance, serving as a blessing and welcoming symbol. We also applied her designs as stencils on the ceiling in the bar area and utilized them as intricate details on the bedding for each room. She also collaborated on creating quilt-like drawings for select bedrooms. These large-scale pieces were meticulously stitched and embroidered by hand, resulting in restful and celebratory wall hangings that harmoniously blended with the project's overall aesthetic. This collaboration with Chris brought forth an unexpected and delightful fusion of tattoo artistry and home design, infusing each space with a unique narrative and visual richness.

CHRIS CASTAÑEDA ↦ CDMX

We encountered Marcela Calderon at a day market hosted by Kurimanzutto Gallery in Mexico City. At her expansive table, adorned with her creations, our attention was immediately captivated. The precision of shapes, the exquisite glazes and vibrant coloring were notable, but what truly stood out were the hand-painted apes and gorillas that adorned some of the ceramic pieces. Executed with a remarkable lightness and a clear mastery of technique, they left a lasting impression on us. Intrigued, we acquired a bowl and began delving more into Marcela's artistic journey. ↵ Marcela was born to a Mexican father and a French mother in Michoacán, and has roots deeply embedded in the rich cultural tapestry of her homeland. Her parents met during a 1970s political movement advocating for land rights in Mexico City, and laid the foundation for Marcela's unique artistic lineage. Her father resided in Patamban, a town that became known in Spanish colonial times for pottery, particularly glazing with lead, and for producing delicate and intricate pieces acknowledged as among the most beautiful ceramics in Mexico. Fired in adobe kilns at low temperatures, these creations possessed a certain fragility. ↵ In the early 1980s, Marcela's parents established a cooperative to push the boundaries of traditional ceramic techniques. They experimented with kilns capable of firing at higher temperatures, revolutionizing the craft. Marcela's father, dedicated to creating patterns for standardized shapes, aimed to empower the community to innovate, producing sturdier pieces that could enhance trade. The outcome was a range of robust vessels suitable for carrying water and storing food. Marcela's upbringing in this ceramic-centric town helped to fuel her aspirations to become an artist. Immersed in a community where nearly everyone was involved in one craft, she spent hours sketching and dreaming. Progressing from paper to ceramic plates, Marcela's early passion centered on drawing animals of various kinds. ↵ Upon relocating to Mexico City for university, Marcela explored various career paths before finding her calling in etchings—precise, graphic drawings with reproducible qualities. Enchanted by the process and results, she became particularly fascinated by era when the printing press was first introduced to Mexico and the early etchings that circulated during that time. Delving into natural history books, she explored representations of European animals, medieval costumes, and narratives that reminded her of her childhood in Patamban. Developing a suite of animals, including foxes, badgers, armadillos, deer, and mountain cats, she wove intricate stories around them, exploring their sexuality and everyday practices, a journaling of sorts. The monkey, symbol of the devil, became a recurring motif in her work. ↵ Marcela's intent was to dismantle the traditional associations animals had with bad omens, reshaping them with narrative into a zoomorphic family that could embody unique characters. It was post-university that she ventured into ceramics, after eschewing the purchase of her own press. She started in Patamban, but concurrently established a thriving studio in Mexico City. Our collaboration has focused on creating wall installations comprised of multiple platters that weave together stories of homes and clients. Through discussions about diverse animals and cohesive groups, we explore avenues to inspire and narrate captivating tales.

HOMES
FOR OTHERS

OJAI
thacher
p.12

Francesca di Mattio is represented by Nina Johnson Gallery, Miami. Sophia Narrett is represented by Michael Kohn Gallery, Los Angeles. Two vintage Amadeo Lorenzato (Brazil) paintings from Gomide & Co, São Paulo, rest on the mantel flanked by a pair of rare vintage Napoleone Martinuzzi cast glass sconces. In the kitchen, the large painting is by Tony de los Reyes and the vintage industrial pendants came from Hollywood at Home, Los Angeles. On the patio, Peter Dunham's "Fig leaf" in pink is used liberally.

HAWAII
las tortugas
p.46

LONG ISLAND
north fork
p.96

There are so many pieces of great collectible design in this project that we could do a separate book. In the sitting room, a rare George Nakashima cabinet from the designer's own home; an upholstered vintage Joaquim Tenreiro sofa from R & Company, New York City with whom our client has had a long relationship; and much of the vintage Brazilian work throughout the house was sourced with the NYC-based gallery. We also work closely with the Paris-based galleries Downtown and Patrick Seguin. RP Miller loves to make quilts from special textiles, we keep a large library of vintage textiles for this purpose as well as inspiration. The wood and leather strapped sofas on the lanai were inspired by Charlotte Perriand designs for Les Arcs in the Alps.

Dokter and Misses is represented by Southern Guild, a gallery working with African artists and designers with spaces in Cape Town and Los Angeles. Thomas Houseago is represented by Gagosian Gallery, New York. David Wiseman works with Kasmin Gallery, New York. Takuro Kuwata is represented by our good friends at Salon 94, New York. The Haas Brothers are represented by Marianne Boesky, New York. RP Miller Textiles are available directly. The vintage Wendell Castle work was acquired through R & Company, New York City. The clients acquired many of the vintage design pieces and art through Phillips and Christie's auction houses over many year of focused collecting.

KENTUCKY
cherokee triangle

There were extensive renovations to the kitchen, back porch and sleeping porches at this house and we were lucky to work with the local architect Thomas Kute. Tommy knew so much about the local vernacular and had been in so many historic homes in the area that his input and vision was invaluable to the project. Marco Rountree Cruz is represented by guadalajara90210, Gaudalajara and CDMX. Gert and Uwe Tobias are represented by Rodolphe Janssen, Brussels. One of our great sources for vintage collectible design is Morentz Gallery, Netherlands. Thaddeus Wolfe is represented by Volume Gallery, Chicago.

KENTUCKY
indian bean

Again at Indian Bean we had the pleasure of working with Louisville based architect Tommy Kute to rework the kitchen and a guest bedroom. Sadly, we have not been able to include images of the fantastic guest room bath he designed for us. In the sitting and dining room custom-colored hand-blocked wallpaper by the British designer Marthe Armitage enlivens the walls. The San Diego–based artist Roy McMakin is represented by Garth Greenan Gallery, New York City. There are numerous installations by Roy on the site not pictured here. Monica Mahoney is based in Louisville.

CAPE COD
truro

The yellow "Dromedary Loveseat" is from John Derian Company, New York City; they have some really great upholstered pieces that we use often upholstered with our own textiles. RP. Miller makes pillows and cushions from collected textiles—vintage, antique and from far-flung locales; they are available directly. Fabien Cappello is represented by AGO Projects, CDMX. The steel and acrylic side tables designed by Rudy are available to order.

MEXICO
hacienda los milagros

Antoine Ratigan of Studio Antoine in Mexico City worked closely with the clients to remodel and establish the architecture of the project. Perla Valtiera is a Mexico-based designer we love and have used her ceramics across this project and others. Hector Zamora is represented by LABOR, CDMX. Claudia Fernandez made the handsome hacienda-style chairs in the dining room. There are wonderful tiles used extensively throughout the project, many of them produced by our frequent collaborators Talavera de la Reyna in Puebla and Ceramica Suro in Guadalajara.

HOMES
FOR OURSELVES

Studio Weiki Somers is represented by our good friends at Galerie Kreo in Paris, one of the best resources for contemporary collectible design. Jim Lambie is represented by Anton Kern, and Tom Burr at Bortolami, both New York City–based galleries; while Milena Muzquiz is represented by Travesia Cuatro in Madrid, CMDX and Guadalajara. Konstantin Kakanias is represented by Gavlak. In this project, as in much of our work, we used a number of great textiles from Pierre Frey, including the incredible dark blue mohair velvet on the sitting room banquette.

We love the work of Assume Vivid Astro Focus and have a number of pieces in Guatemala; AVAF is represented by Casa Triângulo, São Paulo. Naufus Ramírez-Figueroa is represented by Proyectos Ultravioleta, Guatemala City. Gabriel Kuri is represented by Kurimanzutto, CDMX and New York City. Dario Escobar is represented by Nils Stærk, Copenhagen.

Lisa Eisner is an old friend, a fantastic photographer, book publisher and jewelry designer, her photos are available directly. Miguel Calderon is represented by Kurimanzutto, CDMX and New York City. Schweitzer Linen has a number of stores in New York City and also online. Most of the upholstered furniture in the flat was designed and made by RP Miller in our beloved workrooms in Los Angeles.

The vintage dhurry in the sitting room was sourced from Seret and Sons, Santa Fe, New Mexico. The Brazilian artist Erika Verzutti is represented by Fortes D'Aloia & Gabriel, São Paulo. The vintage sofa in the Florida room is upholstered in Mrs. Burnside from RP Miller Textiles. Renate Müller is represented by R & Company, New York City.

Jeffry Mitchell is represented by PDX Contemporary Art. The Nan Goldin photograph was acquired from Mathew Marks Gallery, New York City. Martino Gamper, one of our favorite designers working today, is represented by Nilufar, Milan. The RP Miller textile used for the curtains is Katsuri Flowers in Matcha; it is printed in Los Angeles on Belgian linen.

Gabriel Rico is represented by OMR, CDMX. The contemporary designers Pedro y Juana, Lanza Atelier, Fabien Cappello, Agnes Studio, Anndra Neen, and Fernando Laposse are all represented by AGO Projects, CDMX. Sam Falls is represented by Franco Noero Gallery, Turin. Pedro Reyes's furniture and design work is available through AGO Projects, CDMX.

Acknowledgments

To Noni, Nona, and Nathalie—for always illuminating our path.

We would like to thank the people who supported us in many ways to make this book and our work possible:

Amy Astley, Tatiana Bilbao, Marimar Barrientos, Nina Baier Bischofberger, Toto Bergamo Rossi, Hamish Bowles, Eduardo Braniff, Matus Castillo, Sam Cochran, Malachi Connolly, Tom Delavan, Jennifer Dunlop Fletcher, Peter Dunham, Larry Gagosian, Allison Green, Jeanne Greenberg Rohatyn, François Hallard, Ashton Hawkins (RIP), Alex Heminway, Maja Hoffman, Roman Alonso and Steven Johanknecht, Madeline O'Malley, Lee Keating, Tom Kundig, Allison Levasseur, India Mahdavi, Ana Elena Mallet, Peter Marino, JJ Martin, Karla Martinez de Salas, Hannah Martin, Erik Maza, Barbara Muschietti, Marc Porter, Michael Reynolds, Jorge Rivas, Craig Robbins, Hannah Rothschild, Mayer Rus, Fernanda Sela, Ivan Shaw, Joe Sheftel, Ana Sokoloff, Rupert Thomas, Simon Upton, Stellene Volandes, Sarah Watson, Ari Wiseman; our design wife Paola Aboumrad; the fantastic Vidoun team of Luke P. Brown, Alex Galan, and Tasha Saravia; and our friends Jill Littman and Michael Baum at Impression Entertainment.

To our beloved mothers, Liza and Annelie; our fathers Rodman and Rudy; Karen; our siblings Alix, Kathia, Lory, and Tiky; our stellar nieces and nephews; godchildren; and our extended family, which includes a network of close friends that have always been family.

The photographers we have had the honor of working with, for capturing our world so poetically including Miguel Flores Viana, Gustavo García-Villa, Ben Hoffman, Stephen Kent Johnson, Mary Beth Koeth, Mark Luscombe White, Fernando Marroquín, Manuel Rodriguez, Christopher Sturman, Simon Upton, Dominique Vorillon, and Manolo Yllera.

Ana Karina Zatarain for the introduction, and Michael Snyder for patiently editing all the text in this book.

Our team: Claire Adams, Ana Barbará, Micaela Bentivoglio, Helena Choy, Carlota Coppel, Jan Cox, Alix Jarrard, Genki Matsumura, Santiago Ortiz Monasterio, Amparo Orozco, Elizabeth Padgett, Gloria Paniagua, Amanda Tabush, Antonio Zorrilla, and our AGO Projects family of artists and designers.

A big shout-out to our clients for hiring us, for believing in us, and for wanting to go on these adventures together. To the makers, workrooms, and artists, without whom none of the projects would be possible—thank you!

To the Phaidon/Monacelli team, including Jenny Florence, Stacee Gravelle Lawrence, Michael Vagnetti, and Billy Norwich for making a major dream come true . . . and to the amazing graphic designer Paco Lacasta.

The Authors

RODMAN PRIMACK   Rodman's career began as a junior designer for renowned architect Peter Marino. He moved on to become head specialist in Latin American art for Christie's, and then a director of the Gagosian Gallery in Los Angeles. His impressive background in art and design led to his appointment as executive director and then chairman, London, of the esteemed auction house Phillips de Pury from 2004 to 2010. All the while, he continued to pursue independent design and advisory projects. He is the former executive director and chief creative officer of the international collectible design fair Design Miami. ↵ His passion and deep knowledge of design, craft, contemporary art, and textiles influences and drives all his projects. He is the cofounder of Mexico City–based collectible design gallery AGO Projects. Rodman also sits on the boards of the Tamayo Museum in Mexico City and the International Folk Art Market in Santa Fe, New Mexico.

RUDY WEISSENBERG   Rudy holds a master's degree in design studies focused in art, design, and public domain from the Harvard Graduate School of Design and a master's degree in business administration focused in media management from Columbia Business School of Columbia University. He has combined his interest in media, spending over a decade in both financial and creative roles within large media conglomerates with a passion for art and design, simultaneously curating design exhibitions and advising clients on art and collectible design. He has actively pursued a career in design and works to promote some of the most celebrated contemporary designers. He is currently cochair of the Latin American Circle of Friends of the Guggenheim Museum, New York, and is a member of the Harvard GSD Dean Leadership Council, in Cambridge, Massachusetts, and the board of the Tamayo Museum in Mexico City.

Our interiors practice has an international footprint with a focus on collaborative relationships with architects, artists, and craftspeople. The firm is included on the *Architectural Digest* AD100 list of the world's top design talent, *Wallpaper* US 300, and its work has been published in *T Magazine* of the *New York Times*, *W*, *World of Interiors*, *Vogue Mexico*, *Casa Vogue Brasil*, *Elle Décor Japan*, *Architectural Digest Spain*, and many other publications. Collaboration, cultural amplification, and interesting conversations are the key drivers of the practice.

Photography credits

Gustavo García-Villa: 10–11, 38 top, 38 center, 38 lower right, 40, 41 top left, 41 top right, 41 bottom, 42 top left, 42 top right, 42 bottom, 44 top left, 44 top right, 44 bottom, 45 top, 45 bottom, 60 top left, 60 top right, 60 bottom, 62 top, 62 bottom, 63 top, 63 bottom, 76 top, 76 bottom, 78 left, 78 top right, 78 bottom right, 79 top left, 79 top right, 79 bottom, 80 top, 80 bottom, 82 top left, 82 top right, 82 bottom, 83 top, 83 bottom, 110 top left, 110 top right, 110 bottom, 112 top, 112 bottom, 113 top left, 113 top right, 113 bottom, 114 top left, 114 top right, 114 bottom left, 114 bottom right, 116 top, 116 bottom, 117 top left, 117 top right, 117 bottom, 130 top, 130 bottom, 132 top left, 132 top right, 132 bottom left, 132 bottom right, 133 top, 133 bottom, 146 top, 146 bottom left, 146 bottom right, 148 left, 148 right, 149, 174 top left, 174 top right, 174 bottom, 176 top, 176 bottom left, 176 bottom right, 177, 202 top left, 202 top right, 202 bottom, 204 top, 204 bottom, 205 top, 205 bottom, 218 top, 218 bottom, 220 top, 220 bottom left, 220 bottom right, 221 top, 221 bottom, 242 top left, 242 top right, 242 bottom, 244 top, 244 bottom, 245 top left, 245 top right, 245 bottom, 246 top left, 246 top right, 246 bottom, 248 top left, 248 top right, 248 bottom, 249 top left, 249 top right, 249 bottom ↩ Ben Hoffmann: 84, 86, 87, 88–89, 90–91, 91 inset, 92, 93, 94–95, 95 inset ↩ Stephen Kent Johnson: 163, 164–65, 166–67, 168–69, 169 inset, 170, 171, 172, 173, 206, 208–9, 209 inset, 210, 211, 212, 213, 214, 215, 216 inset, 216–17 ↩ Mary Beth Koeth: 152 inset, 152–53, 156–57 ↩ Fernando Marroquín: 223, 224 inset, 224–25, 226–27, 227 inset, 228, 229, 230–31, 232 inset, 232–33, 234–35, 236–37, 238, 239, 240, 241, ↩ Manuel Rodriguez: 178, 180 inset, 180–81, 182–83, 184, 185, 186–87, 187 inset ↩ Christopher Sturman: 13, 14–15, 16, 17, 18, 19, 20–21, 21 inset, 22, 23, 24, 25, 26, 27, 28, 29, 30–31, 31 inset, 32, 33, 34–35, 35 inset, 36–37, 135, 136, 137, 138, 139, 140, 141, 142–43, 144–45, 145 inset, 189, 190–91, 192, 193, 194 inset, 194–95, 196–97, 198, 199, 200, 201 ↩ Simon Upton, courtesy World of Interiors: 118, 120, 121, 122–23, 123 inset, 124, 125, 126 inset, 126–27, 128, 129 ↩ © VistaBee: 154–55 ↩ Dominique Vorillon: 47, 48–49, 50, 51, 52–53, 54–55, 55 inset, 56, 57, 58–59, 59 inset, 97, 98–99, 99 inset, 100–1, 102–3, 104–5, 104 inset, 106, 107, 108–9 ↩ Mark Luscombe White: 150, 155 inset, 158, 159, 160, 161 ↩ Manolo Yllera: 64, 66 inset, 66–67, 68–69, 70, 71, 72–73, 73 inset, 74, 75

Art credits

Florian Baudrexel © 2024 Artists Rights Society (ARS),
New York / VG Bild-Kunst, Bonn
Jim Lambie © 2024 Artists Rights Society (ARS),
New York / DACS, London
Antionio Segui © 2024 Artists Rights Society (ARS),
New York / ADAGP, Paris
Gert & Uwe Tobias © 2024 Artists Rights Society (ARS),
New York / VG Bild-Kunst, Bonn

Design by Lacasta Design

A Library of Congress Control Number is available
978-1-58093-638-5

Printed in China

Monacelli
A Phaidon Company
111 Broadway
New York, NY 10006
www.monacellipress.com